The
Convent

The Convent

Marie Hargreaves
with Ann and Joe Cusack

MB

MIRROR BOOKS

First published by Mirror Books in 2020

Mirror Books is part of Reach plc
10 Lower Thames Street
London EC3R 6EN

www.mirrorbooks.co.uk

ISBN 978-1-913406-07-3

Typeset by Danny Lyle

Printed and bound in Great Britain by
CPI Group (UK) Ltd, Croydon, CR0 4YY

A CIP catalogue record for this book is available from the British Library.

Every effort has been made to fulfil requirements with regard to
reproducing copyright material. The author and publisher will be
glad to rectify any omissions at the earliest opportunity.

3 5 7 9 10 8 6 4 2

iStockphoto and Arcangel

This book is dedicated to my parents,
Fred and Kathleen, and to my late husband, Jack

Prologue

October 1959.
St Mary's Primary School, Billinge, Merseyside

The wind whipped around the corner of the red brick building and it was bitterly cold – as only a school playground can be. I watched, huddled up at the side of a wet drainpipe, as crowds of kids played hopscotch and jumped in and out of ropes. There were boys kicking a football too, laughing, shouting, their voices carrying on the biting wind. I didn't play. Nobody asked me to play. I wasn't even sure I knew how to play. Not any more.

There were days when, at six years of age, I wasn't even sure what my name was. It was so long since I'd heard it. I was wishing I had a thicker coat, like some of the other kids, when a boy, my age, walked over to me, with the air of someone who had a job to do.

"My big brother wants to go out with you," he said matter-of-factly, nodding his head to the other playground where the next class up were playing.

"He wants to be your boyfriend and he wants an answer."

I was completely taken aback. How had he even noticed me? Me, without a name.

"No, no, no," I replied automatically. "I can't go out with anyone. I'm in the convent."

The little boy nodded, as though he already knew that, and he skipped off with the information. A few minutes later, he reappeared and said: "My brother says he will wait for you.

"When he grows up, he is going to come and look for you, even," – and here he took a big, important, breath: 'Even if you are in Africa!'"

With that he turned on his heel and went back to report to his brother. I stood, rooted to the spot, half impressed, half stunned. Where was Africa anyway? I hadn't a clue, I knew it was a long way away though. But I did know that this was the first show of affection and attention I'd had since losing my home and my family. This was the first time anyone had even spoken nicely to me. And then, and I didn't really understand why, I felt a fat tear rolling down my cheek and splashing onto my battered black shoes. The little boy's kindness had touched and shaped my soul, in a way that no brutality ever could or would.

Years later, as I struggled with flashbacks and memories of the horrors I had suffered at the convent, my wonderful husband, Jack, would take my hand in his and smile: "I'll always love you. I'll come and look for you, even if you're in Africa."

Prologue

That little boy, whose name I never knew, had given me a life-raft. A reason to smile and a reason to feel loved. When all around me was hatred and hostility he was a shining light in a very dark world. And I knew I would remember him for the rest of my life.

Chapter One

There was a yelp, right down my ear, and my big brother, Fred, yelled: "Ow! Mind your bony elbow, our Marie.

"Right in my back!"

I rolled over and away from him, grabbing what scrappy bit of blanket I could to take with me. But I was wide awake now, thanks to Fred bawling down my earhole. And the big bed where we all slept was a tangle of arms and legs. My parents, Fred and Kathleen, were asleep on the other side, with our baby brother, Peter, in-between them. I just couldn't get comfy at all. And Fred was right, my sharp knees and elbows were not welcome here. Not that they were the worst hazard of this set-up, because if one wet the bed, we were all soaked to the skin, and stinking too.

My belly was rumbling, and so, creeping out from under the covers, I made my way across the bedroom, stubbing my toe on the chamber pot, already filled to the brim with the night's pee. I padded downstairs to the small kitchen, which was really just a stone sink and a decrepit old stove, crammed into the far corner of the living room.

Our house, a small, rented terrace in Oldham, was two rooms, one on each floor. We had no carpet and very little furniture and there was a faint smell of damp. Upstairs was the bedroom, where us three kids shared a bed with our parents, the warmth from the thin blankets supplemented by dad's overcoat and the peg rug from the hearth downstairs. Our baby, Christine, slept in a cot at the side of the bed but more often than not, she'd end up sandwiched between the bodies in the bed, too. It was warmer all together. And it was cosy.

Our only toilet, an old-fashioned 'tippler' was outside in the back yard. There was no flushing system. Instead, the waste remained in an open sewer until the tippler was filled with dirty water from the kitchen sink, and it would then tip, sending water through the system to flush away the waste.

I was a skinny, slight, little girl and I lived in mortal fear of falling down into the slimy waters below and drowning in poo.

"Death by poo," Freddie would tell me, his eyes dancing with mischief. "That's what'll happen to you, our Marie."

The yard reeked of sewage – in fact on sunny days, the whole house stank. I could taste the smell on the back of my tongue; feel it stinging my nose. Good job then that in Oldham we had mostly drizzle, and not much sunshine to gag on.

"They should have been condemned years ago, these tipplers," my dad used to say. "We're behind the times."

Chapter One

But for some reason, well into 1955, ours was still tippling and stinking the place out.

In the makeshift kitchen, I was busy rooting in the cupboards for something to eat when mum appeared behind me. She was a tiny lady, maybe 5'1" tall, with jet black hair and a kind, worn face. And although baby Christine was just a few months old, mum's belly was swelling again, with her fifth child in as many years.

"Bread and butter for breakfast Mairin," she told me. "Sorry, love."

She was from Northern Ireland and liked that version of my name. She and my dad were the only ones who used it. Mum had come over from Belfast, looking for work, all alone in the late 1940s. She'd eventually found a job as a hospital cleaner and she and my dad had met in the Star Inn, near our home, and fallen for each other over a pint of Guinness. When Mum was 21, and Dad 36, they got married, and Freddie came along soon afterwards. They moved into Ruth Street, Oldham. Dad had been born there himself and had slept in a drawer by the fireplace.

I liked to imagine that at first, they had been happy and madly in love.

But like everything else in our house, happiness seemed to be in short supply these days. It was still too early for The Beatles to tell the world that Money Can't Buy Me Love. But money could probably have bought me and my family a little bit of fun at least. And some sweets.

3

I'd lie in bed, late at night, and listen to mum and dad bickering and rowing.

"Just a pint, that's all I'm asking!" he would say, in his broad, Oldham accent.

And then mum, her voice rising, and I'd imagine her throwing her hands up: "No way! We've no money, Fred. We've six mouths to feed and another on the way."

The poverty was crippling. On good days, there was enough money to make stew or 'tata 'ash for tea. Bad days, it was jam butties, three times a day. And on really bad days, we got a clip round the ear and an empty belly.

By the age of two, I still couldn't walk and my legs were bowed. Possibly my earliest memory was of pulling myself up at the side of the stove and wondering why my legs were made from soft plasticine, and not bones, like Freddie's. The social workers came and shook their heads in disapproval.

"Your daughter has rickets," they told my mum. "She needs fresh food. Milk. Eggs. She needs sunshine. Days out – away from Oldham."

My mother raised her eyebrows. They may as well have been telling her to put me on a shuttle to the moon.

My diet must have improved a little, for a short time at least, because I eventually learned to walk. Though my legs were always slightly bent and my feet were too flat.

But the poverty was chronic. It was like woodworm, infecting and ruining everything. And a few eggs changed nothing.

There was no money for treats, days out, new clothes. All that belonged in another street and another life. Mum washed the same set of nappies, over and over, year after year, on a board at the sink. When our clothes could no longer be stitched or patched, we'd have a day out at a jumble sale or at Tommyfield Market, to pick up some bargains.

When we arrived at the jumble sale, it was bedlam. There was a swell of bargain-hunters, swearing and shouting and pushing for the front. I was almost lifted off my feet in the middle of the crowd.

And then, somewhere in front, a kerfuffle broke out.

"That's One-Arm Rosie," Freddie told me, giggling on tip-toes. "I can see her from here, whacking people."

One-Arm Rosie was a well-known figure at the jumble sales and her wooden arm, a deadly weapon, was the reason she usually walked away with most of the bargains. She would thump her way to the front, cursing and swearing at the top of her voice.

She was so diminutive that by the end of the sale she would usually be buried under a pile of clothes, bags and shoes.

There was a malevolence about her, which terrified me as a small girl. I used to imagine different scenarios of how she had come by her wooden arm – all equally frightening and far-fetched.

But seeing her smash her way through the crowd, I did wonder whether she'd had her arm cut off, just so that she could be a bully at jumble sales. It worked a treat for her.

Somehow, we squeezed our way through the throng, me, Freddie and Peter, sneaking through people's legs and under their elbows.

I loved trying on all the clothes, piled high on the wooden trestle tables. It didn't matter to me that they were old and musty.

"They're dead people's clothes," Freddie told me with a glint in his eye.

But I stuck my tongue out and paraded round in my new finery. I didn't care. After the jumble sale, it was off to the market. It was freezing, huddled between the stalls with the wind whipping around every corner. I kept an eye on Peter whilst mum shopped.

And I knew it was a good day, because she bought a half-pound of tripe for my dad. It was a delicacy for him. He'd eat it soaked in salt and vinegar, washed down with a tin of ale.

As we traipsed home from our day out, weighed down with cow heel and black pudding, lamb shanks and kidneys, I felt a surge of happiness.

I loved those days out with my mum.

"You're such a good help, Mairin," she told me. "I don't know what I'd do without you, darlin'."

Once a month, we'd load up the baby's pram with washing and go to the washhouse, sitting on the benches alongside all the local women. It was uncomfortably sticky in the wet and the warmth, but the place held a fascination for me. I leaned in, listening to the gossip and the chit-chat. Jaws dropped and eyes bulged.

"Well, I never! Not her! I didn't think she had it in her. Not after the last time."

The stories just got better and better. We couldn't afford to buy a local newspaper or a telly, but then we didn't need one. We had the washhouse.

But our trips were only a temporary escape from the heaviness of life at home. The pressure of being poor weighed on my dear mum. Some days, she was literally bent double with it.

Dad did his best, working on and off as a rag and bone man. He'd trundle down the cobbled streets around our home, shouting "Any old rags! Any old rags!" When I heard his cart, I'd run out into the road in excitement, reaching up to him with my short arms so that he could lift me up and show me what treasures he had collected in his wooden barrow; old bed-spreads, threadbare shirts and skirts, socks with holes in. There was the odd small piece of furniture too, chairs or maybe a little table. Up there, in my dad's arms, I felt like a princess surveying her kingdom. He was poverty-stricken, scruffy and unwashed, illiterate and uneducated, but to me, he was my hero. He made me feel totally safe.

Like me, dad was a chatterbox. He loved telling stories of his days in Burma, during the war.

"We slept on a bed of snakes," he told me and Freddie, as we shrank back in horror. "We fought tigers with our bare hands."

"Wow!" I whistled, my face flushed with admiration.

He had a tattoo of the Taj Mahal on his arm, too.

"I got this in India," he told us. "Four rupees."

Dad grew, as a hero, with every tall tale he told us. I drank in every word. I had questions which lasted until bedtime and beyond, and dad, with endless patience, answered every single one.

"So what hurt more dad, the snakes or the tattoo?"

"And were you not even frightened of the tigers?"

"If you don't ask, you don't learn," dad told me with a smile. "Never stop asking questions, Mairin. Because sometimes, questions are all we have."

It was a lesson I was fast learning.

* * *

Mum couldn't work, not with us children to look after. There was just one year between each of my siblings. She'd hardly have time to get over the birth of one and she'd find herself pregnant again.

Little Johnny, her fifth child, was born in April 1956.

"Every child is a gift from God," she would tell us. "We're grateful for every single one."

But there was no joy in her eyes, no gratitude in her voice, as she spoke. She was a deeply religious Irish Catholic and she turned to the Lord in every crisis, more in hope than expectation.

And sometimes it did feel as though God had forgotten about us on Ruth Street. One time, Freddie and I were playing out in the street, when a large bulldog, with a girl running behind him, launched itself at Freddie. Poor Freddie was so alarmed he bolted into the road without looking. Our street was normally so quiet, but there was a butcher's van making deliveries at that very moment, and I screamed in horror as Freddie went under a wheel and his head hit the cobbles with a sickening smack.

"Freddie!" I yelled.

Dad came running out of the house, baby Johnny, in one arm, and trying to cradle Freddie with the other. I stood, white-faced, dizzy with shock at what I had just witnessed. Freddie was rushed off to hospital, his body limp and pale, and dad, his eyes brimming with tears, tried desperately to reassure me.

"He'll be OK," he promised me. "You wait here with your mum and look after the little ones, Mairin. Hold the fort. There's a good girl."

Dad jumped on a bus, off to the Royal Oldham Hospital, while we waited at home for news.

"Pray for Freddie," mum told us. "Pray to the Lord."

Freddie came home one week later, with his head swathed in bandages. He looked like *The Invisible Man* from the TV series.

Dad was very careful and gentle around him. But mum knocked on the bandages and shouted: "Hello! Anyone home?"

It made her laugh, but not Freddie.

Even at that age, I could see that it wasn't the right thing for mum to find that funny. And I felt a sense of unease and foreboding that I just could not explain. That night, we all had toast before bed, but though my tummy was rumbling, I couldn't stomach anything.

I looked at Freddie's sore head, and I saw mum's smiling face, and I felt sick.

Another time, Peter had climbed onto the kitchen table with Fred and me. We were pretending we were on a trampoline, jumping up and down and screaming in delight. Mum was busy with Christine and Johnny. But in a split second, Peter had toddled off the end of the table, falling with a crash and a crack onto the stone floor.

There was pandemonium! Mum rushed in, screaming and crying. The neighbours came and an ambulance was called and Peter went off to hospital in a wail of sirens. I was just four years old myself, too young to understand the danger, and at first I was excited by the whole episode. I was jealous that I hadn't been allowed in the ambulance myself.

But little Peter had to spend months in Booth Hall Children's Hospital in Manchester. He had a bone taken out of his thigh, and for a while the doctors thought he might even lose his leg. As time went on, and I realised the implications of the accident, I was racked with guilt. After all, I was the eldest girl, the one in charge. Mum was always telling me that she could rely on me.

Chapter One

Why hadn't I taken care of him properly?

It was rare that mum and dad could visit the hospital and I was not allowed to visit at all. We missed Peter terribly. As time went on, he was allowed home visits, but they were occasional and bittersweet. Pleased as we were to see him, there was an awkward tension, knowing he would soon have to return to hospital and leave us all at home. It made my guilt all the worse and I tortured myself for helping him up onto that table.

Each time we waved him off, with tears streaming down our cheeks, we would pray for him to stay safe. Later, when we got a second-hand TV, there was a feature on Booth Hall Hospital on the local news – and there was our very own Peter, in bed, waving at the cameras!

"He's famous!" Freddie shouted. "He's on the telly!"

The little ones ran round the back of the TV to see if they could somehow pull him out. But the whole episode left me strangely sad and empty. To me, it just underlined how far away he was.

Even when Peter came home for good, he wore a brace on his leg and it never completely mended. I was fascinated by the brace and a little envious of it and I wanted one for myself. But Peter had a pronounced limp which slowed him down, and it seemed to both upset and irritate my mum. She would throw her arms around him and then fly at him in exasperation, and sometimes both at once.

"We must ask Our Lord to heal Peter's leg," she would tell us, and we'd all kneel, in a line, on the bare floorboards in the bedroom, feverishly murmuring our way through our prayers.

But my prayers were that mum and dad would stop arguing and that God, if he really was that good, would send some money our way.

Chapter Two

The best thing about our new house was the letterbox. Never in my life had I seen such a contraption and I felt ever so la-di-da, living in a house with our very own shiny letterbox. I loved going outside, poking my hands through and shouting through the gap to Christine. We never got a single letter through the post. To my knowledge, I was the only one who ever used it. But to me, it was a priceless invention. We were officially posh.

Moving house, early in 1958, had been long overdue. The two rooms at Ruth Street could no longer hold us all and the whole row of houses was finally condemned. Right on cue, one year after Johnny, mum had given birth to Jeanie. And with six children, and already another on the way, she was struggling to stay afloat.

Watching her trudge through the days, doing her best but falling painfully short, my heart would ache. And even then, though I was not yet five, I decided that sort of life was not for me. I was not going to have lots of babies when I grew up. My mind was made up.

The new house, on Second Avenue, was on a council estate just outside the town centre, but still just a walk away from the old one. Dad balanced our sideboard precariously on the baby's pram and wheeled it slowly through the streets. The rest of the shabby furniture, what bit we had, was carried, dragged or rolled down the pavements.

The upheaval in the old house upset our resident cockroaches, 'Black Jacks' we called them, and Freddie and me spent the morning alternately chasing and running away from them. I took my shoes off to splatter them, but when it came to the kill, I couldn't go through with it.

The new house, as well as having a letterbox, had a kitchen, an indoor toilet, a bathroom – with a real bath – and three bedrooms. Up until then, we had only ever washed at a sink, or had the occasional scrub down in a tin bath by the fire. And by the time my turn came to use the water, it was already lukewarm and grimy. Hair-washing had been a monthly task. Now, with our very own bath, I could wash my long brown hair just as often as I liked. Such a treat.

Freddie and I ran from downstairs to upstairs and back again, whooping in excitement, our voices bouncing off the walls of the empty rooms.

"We're posh, we're posh!" we yelled, delirious with realisation.

We clattered upstairs again, me twirling round in the bedrooms, Freddie clambering onto the windowsill to look at our new, bigger yard down below.

Chapter Two

"Which bedroom do you fancy, Freddie?" I asked, sucking in my breath. "Which one will you choose?"

But that night, when bedtime came, we were in for a disappointment. Mum tucked all five of us into the double bed which had come from the old house, with baby Jeanie sleeping at the side in a cradle.

"Your dad and I will be up soon," she promised. "Leave us a space."

"What about the other bedrooms?" I asked. "Why can't we sleep in there?"

"We've no more beds," she replied shortly. "No more blankets. It might be a new house, but we still have no money."

A tear rolled down her face as she kissed me goodnight. And as I went to sleep, anxiety and hunger gnawed at my insides. We had a letterbox. But no letters. We had a new house. But this was not a new start. The poverty had followed us here like a bad smell.

It was only weeks after the move that mum's apron was straining against a growing tell-tale bulge and she announced that she was nearing the end of her seventh pregnancy.

"Thank God for every little life, every little soul," she said.

But her voice was weary and a little frightened. Even then, I wondered how we were going to cope. It seemed that there was always a baby to dress, to bathe, to feed. Sometimes, it felt like they were on a conveyor belt, with a different one coming my way every few minutes.

"Mairin – hold the baby! Mairin, burp the baby! Please, Mairin, change the baby!"

She gave birth to Kathleen, her seventh baby in as many years, in March 1958.

It was around this time that we got another bed and the children, except for the babies, now slept in a different bedroom. I was already second in command after mum, and now, in the separate bedroom, I was in charge.

Dad had found me an old doll on his rounds which I named Winifred. It was a name I'd heard once on the radio and I thought it sounded terribly posh. And if I couldn't be posh myself, then I wanted to make sure my dolly had the chance. I realised even then that social mobility was much easier for dolls than little girls.

I never shortened her name to Winnie or Win, because that would have defeated the object entirely. I wanted it to be known that she was posh, and by association, so was I.

Winifred slept on the pillow next to me, with Peter at one side, and Freddie next to him. On my other side were Christine and Johnny.

Bedtimes were a riot. We would tell jokes and play tricks and tickle one another. Mum would come in and sit on the bed and sing Irish lullabies, *Too Ra Loo Ra Loo Ra* and *The Rose Of Tralee*.

She sang rebel songs too: *The Wearing Of The Green* and *Irish Soldier Laddie*.

I'd keep myself awake on purpose, because I loved listening to her sing, mostly because I knew it made her happy. And I was so snug in that big bed. Even so, there wasn't a night went by without someone wetting the sheets, or being sick, or having a bad dream.

But I loved to be the one to step in and cradle little Johnny better, or help change Christine into a new nightie. Dad would tell me I was his "right hand man" and it made me feel ten feet tall.

"Hold the fort, Mairin," he would say.

It was his way of asking me to look after the house whilst he was out. And even though I was not yet five, I relished the responsibility. It was built into me. I even missed school because I was too busy helping out at home.

One day, there was a rap at the door and mum, peering out of the curtains, suddenly froze in horror.

"Mother of God, it's the cruelty man!" she gasped. "Kids, get upstairs!"

We scrambled up the stairs, skinning our knees, as she opened the front door. I heard a big, booming voice, shouting: "Why aren't your children in school?"

I heard mum mumbling excuses and wondered what they could be. She had raised us never to tell lies. And yet, I couldn't see how she could tell the truth, either. We all feared the cruelty man like the child catcher. We knew he brought trouble.

Another morning, mum was exhausted, after a restless night with the babies, and she was fast asleep in bed when the cruelty man came knocking.

Though Freddie was the eldest, I answered the door, assuming what I hoped was a responsible and serious expression.

"Why aren't you at school?" he demanded, leaning forwards so that he towered above me and his grey trousers were almost touching my nose.

"My mum is in bed," I told him truthfully and importantly. "She needs to sleep."

I had expected sympathy for my poor mother, but I was disappointed.

"She needs to send you to school," he retorted. "I'll be back tomorrow. And you had better not be here."

My heart thumped as the door slammed shut. The truth was, I loved going to school. We were warm and well-fed there, we had cartons of milk and hot school dinners. And my teacher, a lovely, gentle lady, had endless patience. I liked her lessons.

"Why, Miss?" I'd ask. "But why?"

I had to question everything. Every sentence, every sum, every rule. But she didn't mind one bit.

One morning, mum was again not well enough to get up early with us, but I was determined to get to school. I searched the house but couldn't find a pair of knickers anywhere, so in the end, I took a small white vest and put my legs through the armholes and tucked the rest into the waistband of my skirt.

Chapter Two

I could feel it slipping alarmingly as I walked to school and I kept one hand on a scrap of cotton, so that it couldn't fall down completely. There was a draught around my nether regions which was not pleasant, but if I sat down all day, I reasoned, I'd be fine. Unfortunately, fate had other ideas.

"Right class, into the school hall," shouted the teacher. "We're going to do some exercise today. Gym kits on!"

My heart seemed to plummet right into my shoes. The rest of my classmates were busy getting changed around me, but I had no gym kit. The rule for anyone without a kit was to exercise in vest and knickers. I felt myself going clammy and tears pricked my eyes. What was I to do? I couldn't announce it, not in front of the whole class. And so, in my own child-like way, I just hoped that nobody would notice. No-one would even remark on the fact that I was wearing a grubby upside down boy's vest – and not a pair of knickers.

And at first, I dared to hope I had pulled it off. We all stood in a line, before fanning out into a circle, and starting to skip. This, of course, was impossible for me. I had to hold up the vest with both hands, whilst covering my modesty, and it was more of an uneven and anxious gallop, than a rhythmic skip.

"Marie!" shrieked the teacher as she spotted my predicament. "There are spare clothes in the lost property box. For heaven's sake child, go and find a pair of knickers!"

The idea of wearing someone else's knickers was shaming enough. But the sniggers of my classmates, as I left the hall, cut right through my heart and would live with me forever.

When I got home that afternoon, mum was still feeling under the weather and I had no time to change out of the borrowed knickers, because there were babies to cuddle and nappies to change.

It wasn't that our mother was lazy or disinterested, and I had no doubt at all that she loved us dearly. Back then, she was dismissed as a little difficult, a little unstable. Looking back now, I feel sure that she suffered with a crippling post-natal depression – undiagnosed and untreated. And with each baby, it just got worse and worse. She seemed to be sinking – drowning – in a thick sludge of despair.

Relatives would confide in me, much later in life, that there was a strain of mental illness running through mum's family. Several of her relatives had been diagnosed with schizophrenic conditions. She struggled on, one pregnancy after another, and the light in her eyes dimmed with every new addition.

Much as she lived for her children, we were slowly killing her, too.

* * *

It didn't help that dad's mum, Fanny, lived in the next street and she would often call at the house. From as far back as I could remember, she had disliked my mum. The two of them clashed all the time. Fanny would criticise the way mum looked after us, the way she kept her house. It was sad, because of course all of mum's family, including her own mother, who was known as Annabelle, were in Belfast. She was completely isolated, and my paternal grandmother could have been a source of support for her. But for whatever reason, that wasn't to be.

"These children need feeding, Kathleen," my granny rapped. "And when was the last time you washed your windows I wonder?"

Like my mum, Fanny was a tiny woman, but also like mum, she had a temper. And one day, when their bickering spilled over, Fanny picked up her walking stick and hit my mother on the arm with it. Dad rushed to intervene, probably more frightened, I think, of mum retaliating than of granny hurting her. He steered granny smartly out of the house, but mum was seething and the truce between them, from then, was fragile at best.

"It's my house," she told my dad afterwards. "I won't be attacked under my own roof. You tell her. She's your mother. You sort her out."

Poor dad was stuck in the middle and if he sought solace in a pint down at the Star Inn, he got in trouble for that, too. He was a placid, quietly-spoken man and I think he was probably quite frightened of the fearsome women in his life.

Mum's temper, or her illness, whatever it was, flared up shortly after another fractious visit from our gran. She and dad had been arguing, as usual, over money – or the lack of it.

"Look!" yelled my mother, grabbing her purse and shaking a few, pathetic coppers onto the bare floor. "How can I feed them with this?"

Her words were desperate and loaded with accusation. Her eyes shone with a madness I hadn't seen before and instinctively, I stood behind my father. We watched, trans-fixed with horror, as mum picked up an ornament and threw it at the window. She was only a small woman. But what she lacked in size she made up for in oomph and the window smashed and shattered into a million shards.

The little ones screamed in delight, thinking it was some sort of game. But I stood, frozen and aghast.

Dad paused for a moment before turning on his heel and slamming out of the house. There was silence, except for muffled, shuddering, sobs and I realised it was me, I was crying.

Mum sank onto a chair, deranged but defeated.

"Me and Freddie will clean it up," I babbled. "Don't worry, mummy. We'll sort it out."

Freddie was already in the back yard, searching around for a board and some nails. In the end, he borrowed a hammer and a sheet of wood from a neighbour and waited for dad to come back and help him fix the hole. Inside the house, I was busy keeping the little ones away from the splinters of glass, whilst I swept up what I could with a dustpan and brush.

"You're a good girl, Mairin," mum said softly.

That night, and the next, I cried myself to sleep, and I prayed harder and harder for help to come. And, just a few days later, it actually seemed as though my prayers might have been answered.

A knock at the door and two social workers stepped into the living room. One carried a bag of sweets and little toys and we dived on them like seagulls after a bag of seaside chips.

"Mine! Mine! Mine!"

But as always, I had one eye on the visitors. And to my dismay, as they spoke with mum, she collapsed onto a chair and began to sob.

"I can't feed my children," she wept, picking at the skin around her fingernails. "I don't have any money."

One of the visitors marched into the kitchen and theatrically swung open the cupboard door. Sitting on the shelf, all by itself, was one lonely Oxo cube.

"Of course you can feed your children!" she said.

And with that, they swept from the house, leaving my mother crying to herself.

It seemed to me that the new house had brought us nothing but worry and bad luck. The poverty was sanitised, but it was as real and depressing as it had always been. We had three bedrooms, but one of them was empty. We had a nice kitchen, but the cupboards were bare.

* * *

My fifth birthday came, in July 1958, and there was no fuss at home. Mum and dad never had any money to spend on our birthdays and even at that age, I did not kid myself into thinking there might be a present. It just wasn't how things were in our family.

But the house was too busy for me to dwell on that for long. And when the little ones gathered around and sang Happy Birthday, through their lisps and their missing teeth, I beamed with happiness.

Mum stood a little way back, glassy-eyed and distracted. She didn't refer to my birthday in any way.

It was hard, not even having a cake, or a homemade card. Especially amongst other kids of my age. It was lucky that my birthday fell during the school holidays, so that at least I didn't have to explain to the other kids what I didn't get for my big day.

But as soon as I went back, in September, the teasing began. It was relentless. I was sick of the way I was singled out. Ever since the day I'd gone in without knickers, I was known as the kid with no money.

"You've no money for clothes," they jeered. "No money for food."

They laughed at my bow legs too, a legacy from my poor diet. I didn't cry, I gave as good as I got. One day, a girl pulled my hair because she said she hated poor people.

Chapter Two

"Now I'll pull your hair even harder!" I yelled.

And I made sure that I did, as well. But, deep down, the shame ate away at me. I longed to show them, to make them take back their taunts. For once, just for once, I didn't want to be "poor Marie."

One morning, I was busy getting ready for school, mum was in bed, unwell, and I spotted her purse on the kitchen table. Without really thinking ahead, I unzipped it and there, nestling in-between the small change, was a crisp ten-shilling note.

"Wow!" I gasped.

I felt like Charlie Bucket with a golden ticket. Stuffing the note into my knickers, all I could think of was my friends' faces, dripping with envy, when they saw how rich I was. I skipped off to school, and on my way I stopped at the corner shop and bought the biggest bar of Dairy Milk I could find. All day long, the chocolate sat in my bag, like smuggler's treasure. And then, at the bell, I pulled it out, like a rabbit from a hat, and the other children swarmed around me.

"Ooh, look what Marie's got."

"Where did you get that? Who gave it to you?"

"Bought it myself," I replied, trying to act casual as I snapped blocks off and shared them around the group. There was enough left for me to have a whole strip to myself too.

The chocolate was heavenly. We didn't get treats much at all and I savoured every last luxurious mouthful.

I skipped home feeling absolutely wonderful. The chocolate had given me a boost, right down to my toes. But when I walked in through the front door, my guilty mouth smeared with chocolate, mum and dad were waiting. Instantly, I began to tremble, awash with regret.

"Why did you do it?" dad asked. "That's a lot of money, Mairin. It's an awful lot of money."

"I didn't want to be poor," I replied, knowing, even as I spoke, how pathetic and selfish that sounded.

"Don't do it again," he said softly. "And we'll say no more about it."

But the sight of my mother, with her head in her hands, mute with despair and disappointment, was worse than any punishment.

Chapter Three

That Christmas, there was very little festive spirit in the house. We had another visit from charity workers, who brought a bag of toys for us all. But they were unwrapped and so we could clearly see the dolls and the toys inside.

"You have to wait until Christmas," dad told us, hiding the bag away.

We spent the next few days searching the house for the bag, and so of course, by Christmas morning, there were no surprises left. Even so, we were whipped up into a frenzy, just like most kids. In the afternoon, we decided to put a Christmas play on for our parents. I dragged sheets and blankets off the bed and found a tea-towel in the kitchen. Freddie and Christine played Mary and Joseph and I threw a blanket over my head and hee-hawed like a donkey. My parents laughed and cheered as we paraded round the living room and my heart was filled with warmth. Maybe, just maybe, there was hope for the future after all.

But the New Year of 1959 brought biting cold and driving rain, and business was bad for rag and bone men.

There were more rows, more fights. The social workers came back and inspected the kitchen once again. And in school, my worried teachers would ask questions.

"Have you had breakfast, Marie?" they asked me. "Is your Mummy OK or is she in bed?"

I wasn't old or wise enough to give them the wrong answers. I was the right hand man, after all, at home. I told myself I was capable of answering anything they asked.

And so the stress built – and built. It felt like a boil, growing, bulging, waiting to be burst.

There was another visit from the social workers. And then, the police came round too. We were sent upstairs whilst the officers spoke to my parents, but we sat on the bottom step and listened, holding our breaths.

"Complaints of rows… loud noise and furniture being knocked over… children in the house…"

"This just won't do."

The tension in the house was so thick, I could taste it on the back of my tongue.

Easter arrived and it was traditional, round our way, to dress up in Easter bonnets and in our best clothes, and to knock on the neighbours' doors. They would – hopefully – gasp in admiration and hand over a few pennies.

But this year there was no money for bonnets, not even second-hand ones. I couldn't bear to see the little ones go without. Their disappointment was worse even than my own.

So one afternoon, when mum was busy with baby Kathleen, I took Christine and Jeanie out to play and I came up with a plan. It wasn't far to the nearest row of shops, and I had seen some lovely Easter bonnets on a display inside. Sneaking in, all we could see were the legs and the skirts and the shopping bags of the adults around us. In my naivety, I felt we were blending in, as though nobody would notice three filthy kids without a penny to their name.

But my mind was fixed firmly on the bonnets. I spotted them, on a stand, as lovely as they were unattainable.

"Here!" I hissed to Christine. "Get ready."

As soon as the sales assistant turned to speak to a customer, I popped three bonnets onto three waiting heads, my own included, and Christine and I scarpered from the shop, as fast as our skinny little legs could carry us. Jeanie toddled along behind, blissfully unaware of her part in the crime, and I had to scoop her up in my arms. My heart was banging so loudly I thought the noise of that alone would give us away. We ran and ran, without stopping, our bonnets on our heads, until we reached the front door. Turning round I fully expected to see a line of policemen behind us – but there was nobody.

"We did it!" I whooped triumphantly.

That Easter, we collected a whole bag of pennies and sweets and apples to share amongst the family. It was wonderful to see everyone smiling as we divided the spoils and I consoled myself that although I had done a bad thing, it had been for a good reason.

And that surely God would understand.

I got into a worse scrape soon after, when I was again playing in the street, this time with a girl much older than me. We had looped a rope swing over a tree on some wasteland nearby, when we spotted a man taking a leak behind a shed.

"Ask him to show us his Thing!" she whispered.

I had a streak of mischief and I couldn't resist a dare. I was keen to impress the bigger girl, too.

"Hey Mister! Show us your Thing!" I yelled, dissolving into giggles. To our astonishment, he turned and showed us, and in panic we raced to my friend's house where her older brothers were in the middle of a meal.

Outraged, they stormed out into the street to search for the man. When they couldn't find him, the police were called and, as a squad car pulled up outside our home, my sense of mischief suddenly withered. A stern WPC announced she would take me on a tour of the surrounding streets to see if we could find the flasher.

"What did he look like?" she asked. "And what was he wearing?"

But my mind was a worrying blank. I remembered a sort of jacket, with an emblem on the front. But apart from that, I was a little hazy. I was just a little girl, after all.

And, as we trawled the streets, I discovered, bizarrely, that every man we came across looked just like him.

"Could be him, or him, or him," I said enthusiastically. "And it could be him!"

We finally reached the police station and the WPC sat me down, picked up a pen and paper, and asked: "What exactly did you say to him?"

"I told him to show us his Thing," I replied, with a straight and serious face.

"I need to know what you mean by Thing," she explained. "You need to be clear."

But once again, I was convulsed with giggles, and bright red with embarrassment, and try as I might, I could not say the word.

"It's too rude," I sniggered. "I can't."

I couldn't even bring myself to write it down, and anyway, I wasn't sure of the spelling. She gave up in the end but I got a ride home in a police car, to mark the end of a very exciting day.

Little did I know, I wouldn't be laughing so much again for a long time to come.

* * *

One evening, with dad off in the pub, mum worked herself up into a frenzy. And when his face appeared at the doorway, she flew out of her chair and swiped everything off the sideboard.

The sound of the dainty little ornaments smashing onto the floor broke my heart. They were so precious to me.

I'd found them at one of the jumble sales; an ornamental teapot, milk jug and sugar bowl, all in the shape of little cottages, and I adored them.

As the row raged around me, I found the dustpan and brush and quietly swept up the fragments. They were nothing special. Except to me.

One afternoon soon after, all us kids were huddled round the old telly dad had picked up on his rounds, but he and mum were rowing so loudly it was hard to hear.

"We've no money!" mum shrieked. "The kids need shoes, Fred. It's raining outside, the roads are wet through, and their shoes are full of holes.

"Where's my purse? I'll show you what money we have!"

On it went, in the background, like white noise. Mum was flinging things around, looking for her missing purse. We were used to it and, unconcerned, turned up the TV volume. But suddenly, I caught sight of a flash of silver, and Dad let out a scream.

"You stabbed me!" he cried, holding onto his arm.

There was blood, all over his hands, as he staggered backwards, sickly with shock. Mum, with a pair of scissors in her hand, fled into the street and screamed for help. Dad went off in an ambulance, all on his own, and we watched, panic-stricken, wondering if we would ever see him again.

"Kneel and pray," mum pleaded. "Pray that your father will be OK."

Chapter Three

I had never prayed so hard in my life. Long after we were allowed to get up from the cold floor, I was mentally running through the *Our Father* and the *Hail Mary*, over and over. How many would it take to save him? In bed, I tried to broker a deal with God, my dad's life in exchange – for what? What did I have that I could give him?

"I'll work hard and look after the little ones," I promised silently. "I won't ask for anything. I'll say extra prayers. Please make sure my dad is OK."

I was still wide awake, late that night, when the door opened quietly and I heard dad's voice downstairs. Weeping silent tears of gratitude, I fell into a restless sleep, and wondered how – or if – we would get through this latest disaster.

Chapter Four

One morning, at the end of August 1959, a good 18 months after we moved to the new house, mum and dad called us all into the living room. It was a Monday, and the last lazy days of the summer holidays, so we would normally be allowed to run around in our nighties and pyjamas. But this morning, dad had insisted on us all getting dressed. We weren't allowed to play out either. It was unusual, but not enough to ring alarm bells.

Dad wasn't out with his cart, either. But again, that wasn't especially out of the ordinary. He didn't work every day, and not if it was raining. Today, though, was bright and clear.

"Come on children," he shouted up the stairs. "Come and sit down here with us."

We had a mottled green suite, second hand and donated no doubt either by customers on dad's round or the various charities who seemed to prop up our family structure.

Fred and I sat on one couch with my mother, surrounded by the little ones and with a baby on her knee, on the other couch. I felt a short sting of resentment that there was no room for me next to mum. Not anymore. She was too busy with the little ones – they were too noisy, too needy. I was six years old and I was the grown-up now.

Dad paced the room, anxious and quiet for a change. There was an expectant, prickly, sort of atmosphere.

"What's happening, dad?" I asked.

He stopped and looked at me, and there was so much tenderness in his eyes, so much love in his face, that I felt almost unsettled. What was going on? It was the sort of look you might give a family pet before having it put down.

"We can always rely on you, Mairin, to ask a question," he said eventually, with a sad sort of a smile.

"Yes, dad, but what's going on?" I pressed. "Why are we all stuck in this room?"

He sighed heavily.

"There's someone coming for you," he replied, pacing again.

I opened my mouth to ask another question, but baby Kathleen began to cry and Johnny started pulling at dad's trousers, demanding attention. And so, I closed my mouth again. I knew my place. I was big now.

We were waiting. Watching. For what?

It seemed like an age before dad cleared his throat, nodded towards me, and said: "There's a car here for you."

Our heads bobbed up in excitement. It was a rarity to even hear the noise of an engine on our street. We would run after cars to see who was inside, hopeful they might chuck out a few coins or sweets. I'd never been in a car in my entire life. So what on earth was one doing here?

Freddie hung back, I noticed, but then he'd always been wary of cars, ever since his accident with the butcher's van. The little ones ran to the window, chattering and bickering for the best vantage spot. But I was transfixed; stunned by the privilege. All my life, I had been one of many, learning to make way for little ones, putting their needs before mine.

And now – for the first time ever – it was all about me.

"For me?" I repeated in awe.

Dad nodded but didn't meet my eye. And in that split-second, I faltered a little.

"Come on," he said briskly, sharply even. "For you and Freddie."

Another flash of unease. Dad hurried us to the front door and, without even a backward glance at my mother, we were in the hallway. Dad handed me my grey coat – another jumble sale triumph, won in a stand-off with One-Arm Rosie. Freddie buttoned his up, too, and put on his shoes.

"Where are we going?" I asked, confusion creeping in.

"You're going on your holidays," Dad smiled. "You and Freddie."

There was no smile in his eyes, I noticed, but I didn't dwell on that. I looked at him in amazement, and as the words sank in, I felt a rush of excitement. I had never in my entire life been away on holiday.

"Freddie!" I beamed. "We're off on holiday! You and me!"

Dad opened the front door and there were two well-dressed ladies stood outside. Not from round here, I told myself. That was for sure.

They wore woollen coats, pleated skirts, and smart shoes with small heels.

"Well, if these are the ladies from the holiday place, it must be posh," I thought to myself.

I had a moment of regret that Winifred was lying upstairs, forgotten, in the bed. If it was a posh holiday, I was sure she would like to come with me.

"Can I go and get Winifred?" I began.

But then dad gave us a gentle push out onto the pavement and one of the women opened the car door.

"Hop inside," she said.

The other took her place at the driver's side and switched on the engine.

Winifred would just have to wait until I got home and told her all about it. I sank onto the leather seats like Thumbelina on a huge, soft cushion. It smelled, to me, of posh. Just the kind of car which suited perfectly a family with a letterbox. Well, what a holiday this was going to be.

As we pulled out of the street I craned my neck through the back window, dying to spot anyone I knew. I wanted them to see me, in the car, going on holiday! This was big news. This knocked spots off handing out chocolate at school. This was proof, at last, that we were rich after all. But, just my luck, there wasn't a soul about.

"Typical," I muttered to myself. "Everyone is missing my big moment."

It was annoying. There was no one to drool with jealousy, nobody to report back to all my school-friends. Nobody to witness just how our luck had changed.

But as we reached the end of the street, I spotted dad, slinking back into the house, and closing our green front door, without so much as a wave.

It was another moment of disquiet. But then I looked around the car, and at Freddie sitting quietly next to me, in his short pants, his shirt and braces, and his tatty coat, and I was flooded with enthusiasm again.

"We're off on our holidays," I said to Freddie. "Can't wait. Can't wait. Can you?"

But Freddie just looked at me, his face a mixture of upset and suspicion. And he said nothing.

True, we had no suitcase. But then, we didn't have many belongings anyway. Maybe it was the sort of holiday where the clothes were included. The fact was, I didn't really know what a holiday was. I had no idea what to expect. I just knew it would be fun.

I did think that perhaps mum and dad might have been a bit more pleased for us. But then, I reasoned, they were probably jealous, just like everyone else would be. We were the first in the family to go away on a holiday – the first ones to even go in a car – and I for one was determined to make the most of it.

* * *

We seemed to fly through the dreary streets of Oldham and the houses and factories soon gave way to countryside.

"Look at the trees, Freddie!" I gasped. "And the cows! Real cows!"

We had never in our lives been out of Oldham. I had never even seen a real cow. It was one unusual experience after another, a bombardment of the senses, a treat. A real treat.

"Might be off to the seaside," I said to Freddie. "Might be a caravan! Or a hotel!"

But as we drove on, the clouds darkened and the day, which had started sunny and warm, turned overcast and gloomy. And already, a very small part of me was missing home.

With my nose pressed against the window, I concentrated on looking out for the sea.

"Might be on your side, Freddie," I reminded him. "It'll be like a big blue bath. Shout if you see it."

Freddie didn't reply. He had never been so quiet in his whole life. The two women in the front murmured quietly to each other, but didn't say a word to Freddie or me. But I had faith in them, because they were so posh. And they smelled wonderful too, clean and fragrant – and dry. Our house was musty and damp, and we all smelled a little like we hadn't quite dried out properly. So I liked this new, hygienic smell.

"'S'cuse me," I ventured. "Do you know when we'll be arriving at the holiday place?"

The woman in the passenger seat turned and said: "Not long, dear."

Ever the chatterbox, I was on a roll now.

"I've a dolly called Winifred," I told her.

Because Winifred was a posh name, I thought this might impress her. But she just ignored me and turned back around without even a reply. And I was left thinking of my Winifred, lying on the pillow, all on her own at home. I hoped Christine would look after her for me, until I was back.

After what seemed like an age, the car slowed and turned into a gravelly drive. I could hear the tyres crunching on the pebbles and I knew we must be near the sea.

But when the car finally stopped, it was outside a magnificent stone building.

"It's a mansion," I said to Freddie, my eyes widening in wonder. "It's a mansion by the sea."

Apart from those three words, neither of the two women had spoken to us throughout the whole journey, but again, I thought they were probably jealous. We were off on holiday, and they weren't. It was all I could do to stop myself chanting and singing and thoroughly rubbing their noses in it.

But now, one came to open the car door and we stepped outside, not onto pebbles exactly, but a sort of gravel.

"This way," she smiled, and she took my hand.

We walked up stone steps – too wide for my tiny legs – to huge oak front doors, which seemed to glare down at us, and creak in complaint as they opened slowly.

A nun, in a floor length black habit, stood at the other side. I was not expecting this at all. I caught my breath. In my child's mind I wondered if her dress was that long because she didn't have any legs. Half nun, half vulture. She had a mouth so thin, so mean, it looked like a slash wound. And it did not smile as she gestured us inside with an already impatient wave.

She was not old. Probably not as old as my mother. But she had a haughty, imperious air and a tight face without a trace of kindness. Her features were so sharp I thought she might cut me if she put her face near mine.

And I realised, as her thin lips tightened, that this was no holiday. Instinctively, I reached out for Freddie.

"Come this way," she ordered.

For a split second, I thought about making a run for it. Could I find my way home? Could I shout and scream for help? But what about Freddie? I couldn't leave him here. So we stepped inside the dark, scary doorway.

Chapter Five

We found ourselves in an entrance hall, cavernous and cold, gloomy, with a highly polished wooden floor. And on a plinth, a statue of the Virgin Mary gazed benevolently down at all God's children. The fear was so real I could touch it, taste it. I heard Freddie whimper a little, like a frightened puppy, at the side of me.

Rooted to the spot, I heard the big doors crashing shut, with an ominous finality. And, in the distance, I heard the car we had arrived in, driving away, over the gravel, until it faded to nothing.

My heart was thumping. Our holiday and all its promise had melted away like warm ice-cream. What was going on?

I had so many questions tumbling over each other in my head that, perversely, I said nothing. I couldn't find the words.

The nun was already sweeping down a corridor and barking at us to follow. She walked briskly and my short legs, as I trotted after her, could barely keep pace. The corridor was dark but every now and again a shaft of multi-coloured light, refracted through the stained glass windows, would burst through, making a weak kaleido-scope on the wooden floor. They were pretty patterns and despite myself, I smiled. But as she saw me pause for a moment, the nun reached out and pinched my arm hard. I squealed in protest.

"Oi!" I yelped. "My arm!" I felt tears pricking the back of my eyes.

My heart began thumping as we were led into a small office and a door closed behind us.

"Mother Superior, here they are," said the nun smoothly. "The Kibblewhites."

Another nun, ancient, older I reckoned, than my own granny, was sitting behind a desk. She looked us up and down for a moment and there was half a smile around her lips. Her face was so craggy with lines ploughed by prayer that I could barely see her eyes. But there was a kindness, a softness, to her that the first nun certainly didn't have. She was plumper too, and I liked that. It was familiar and made me think of my Irish granny.

For a few minutes, she was busy writing and I gazed steadily in front of me at a huge bookcase, lined with thick, dusty-looking books. There was another statue too, this time of Jesus, holding his bloodied heart in his own hands. It was the sort of image which might ordinarily scare a little girl. But the statue didn't scare me half as much as the nun standing behind me.

Eventually, the elderly nun put down her pen, looked up, and said: "Welcome to Our Lady's Convent. You will be here for some time."

"Why?" I asked, unable to help myself. "And where is the sea, please?"

There was a sharp intake of breath behind me and I could almost feel the white-hot anger from the younger nun, burning the back of my neck. But Mother Superior just inclined her head and said quietly: "I hope you are going to be good."

It wasn't in me to succumb so easily, and I shook my head firmly. But I didn't speak again.

"Sister Isobel, will you take the girl?" asked Mother Superior.

The door opened, and I felt another sharp pinch as I was yanked, by my arm, back out into the corridor. Freddie was left behind, silent and downcast, as I was steered off down a new passageway. I tried to look back, to see if he was all right, and I saw another nun talking to him.

But then, the corridor turned a corner, and I lost sight of them both.

Surely though, it was my job to speak up? It was always my role; with the cruelty man, with the police, with the teachers. At six years of age, I was a mini-matriarch. I was always the one with the voice. Now was the time to use it.

Chapter Five

"Where am I going?" I demanded. "And where is my brother?"

Sister Isobel did not speak and her face was set, like angry plaster.

There was a high archway at the end of the corridor and the only sound, as we walked towards it, was the sharp tap tap of her shoes on the polished parquet floor.

"Why I am here?" I asked, braver now, louder.

When there was no reply, I held back, digging my heels in like a frightened foal. But Sister Isobel just gripped me even more tightly and dragged me, my shoes squeaking on the wooden floors, further into the gloom. There were no windows here and no pretty patterns. Abruptly we turned off into a large, cold bathroom, with a row of baths and, through another archway, a row of sinks. There was a strong, anti-septic smell of carbolic soap. And the ancient pipes along the walls, were already grumbling and gurgling in protest at what was to come.

* * *

In the next minute, four or five girls, maybe aged 12 or 13, appeared in the bathroom.

Still, a small, silly, six-year-old part of me was expecting the holiday to start. So maybe these girls would be the ones to take me to the sea?

"Scrub her!" rapped Sister Isobel.

"Aw," smiled one of the girls, taking in every inch of my grey coat, my waist-length hair, and my black shoes. "In't she lovely? What's 'er name then?"

Sister Isobel was already out of the door, but her voice rang out, cold and mocking, from the corridor.

"Kibby. Her name is Kibby."

"My name isn't Kibby!" I exclaimed, more in surprise than anger.

Perhaps it was from my surname, Kibblewhite. But that wasn't my name. That wasn't me.

A hopeful bit of me wondered whether perhaps there was a mix-up. Maybe a little girl named Kibby had gone off to the seaside – and I was stuck here by mistake in her place.

"Not me," I explained again. "I'm called Marie. You've got the wrong girl."

But they just giggled and cooed at me like I was a new kitten.

With the bath running, the girls snatched at my shoes, pulling off my socks, unzipping my clothes. I was plonked in the bath and they began pawing at me and stroking me as though I was a new and exotic pet.

"Aw, in't she gorgeous," leered one girl greedily.

"She is, yeah, she's cute," drawled another.

They all gathered around the bath, feeding off my fear, oohing and aahing with sinister smiles. I felt like a freak show. Their faces were so close I could feel their warm, milky, breath. They didn't smack their lips and rub their hands together, but they might as well have. They were pretty girls, with clear complexions and soft curls in their hair. And they had nice white teeth, which they bared as they smiled.

"I want to see Freddie," I said defiantly. "And I want my mum."

But nobody was listening.

"Sit down, Kibby," they said. "Sit down in the water."

But I remained standing, ready to make a run for it. I didn't want to sit down. Not here. I didn't want a bath. But these girls were so much older than me. There was no chance I could outrun them. I was powerless, helpless. And though I was standing up in the water, I felt as though I was gasping for air.

I shrank back, as though scalded, as one scrubbed me and another washed my hair. Then, I was hoisted out and towelled down and dressed in someone else's vest and knickers, a small navy skirt and a horrible, scratchy woollen jumper which felt as though it was made of barbed wire. My skin felt red raw. Inside and out.

"Why are you doing this?" I asked, bewildered. "Why am I here?"

There were no answers. They pulled and pushed me, dried and dressed me, as though I was a doll. At six, I was used to being in authority at home; outspoken and bossy. Here I was nobody. Nothing.

I grabbed my old clothes from the floor and held them tight. I would need these, when I was back to being somebody again. When I got home.

Next, I was taken into another, smaller room and one of the girls said: "You're having your hair cut now, Kibby."

I stared in horror.

"I'm not Kibby and I don't want my hair cut," I whimpered. "Please."

I had lovely long brown hair; I was proud of it. The big girls had lovely long hair too – so why did they want to cut mine? I would look back and wonder whether this was some sort of cruel initiation ritual, a baptism of evil in a cathedral of Catholic suffering.

In the next minute a new nun appeared carrying an impossibly large pair of shears and I was pushed into a wooden chair. She began clacking at my hair as though I was an unruly privet hedge. Silent tears of shock and loss rolled down my face as clumps of hair floated to the floor. Then she used manual clippers to shave it close to the skin, pinching the nape of my neck. I could feel my hair falling away, high above my ears, way above my forehead.

"D'ya feel like a boy, Kibby?" shrieked one of the girls gleefully. "Do ya? Ya look like a boy but do ya feel like one, eh?"

I shook my head, numb with trauma. I had no words left. I didn't feel like a boy. Truth was, I didn't even feel human.

* * *

From the bathrooms, with a girl at each side, I was taken back through the corridors, and into a huge dining room, filled with round tables, and with five or six girls at every table.

"Kibby you sit here," said one of the older girls, pulling out a chair.

"My name's not Kibby," I choked, angry tears stinging my eyes.

I sat down anyway, with the other children staring at me in interest. We seemed to be on the youngest table, we were sorted in order of age. But I was the youngest. And definitely the smallest.

Over the other side of the room were the boys, again sitting around circular tables. I scanned the faces, looking for Freddie. I wanted so desperately to see him but I was ashamed, too, of my hair. What would he think? Would he even recognise me?

There were nuns all around the edge of the room, and when one bellowed "Quiet!" every head fell forwards, and each small pair of hands was joined in prayer. It was almost like clockwork, like she had flicked an imaginary switch.

"For what we are about to receive, may the Lord make us truly thankful!" she shouted.

She did not sound at all thankful and I was tempted to say just that to the girl sitting next to me. But instead, I bowed my head and closed my eyes, just like everyone else.

Then there was a scraping of chairs as we joined a long queue for bread and butter. We were each given a cup and then we queued again, this time in front of a nun with a white jug, filled with milk. But I was somewhere between horror and terror and I could not bear to eat anything.

The nuns stood over us, watching like crows in their long black habits, with beady eyes and sharp beaks, waiting and hoping for someone to fail.

After the bread was finished, there was mayhem again, and the children seemed to disappear in all directions.

Sister Isobel stepped forwards and said: "Take Kibby to her dormitory," and the same gang of girls surrounded me once again. Like a little lamb, on the way to the abattoir, I walked wearily, head down, flanked by my captors. I was tired now, exhausted by the stress.

We went up a flight of stone steps, along more endless corridors, where on each windowsill was a statue: The Virgin Mary, The Sacred Heart, St Teresa.

"Help me," I whispered. "Help me, please."

But nobody was listening. Not the statues, and certainly not the girls. They chattered away around me, over my head.

"I'll put your rollers in for you after this," squawked one. "He'll notice if you curl your hair, oh he will."

They dissolved into peals of laughter.

"If you hitch up your skirt he'll notice you even more," giggled another.

I kept my head down. I didn't understand what they were saying, and I didn't want to. Although they were pretty, I felt such a strong sense of mistrust. And yet they hadn't exactly been unkind to me. They smiled and cooed all the time, but there was something sarcastic in the way they fussed over me. Something malevolent in their white smiles.

"Here we are, Kibby," said the first girl, as she opened a door into a small, windowless room. There were two beds, one just a bare mattress, and a small table with a locker beneath, in-between them. On the table, was a set of rosary beads – small, brown beads like polished berries.

"Those are yours, Kibby," said the second girl. "Aren't you a lucky thing, eh?"

That made them all laugh again and it made me think I was anything but lucky.

At the bottom of the first bed was a nightdress, so starchy that when one of the girls picked it up, it seemed to stand up on its own. While they were distracted, making fun of my nightdress, I threw my old clothes from home under the bed.

Then the girls pulled off my itchy wool jumper and instead forced the stiff nightdress over my head. It felt a cheese-grater, taking with it a layer of skin from my face.

But I said nothing.

They spun me round and tied the nightdress firmly at the back.

"You wait here, Kibby," they told me. "Wait until the prayer bell rings."

And with that, they were gone, leaving me trussed up like a tiny, frightened, ghost. On the wall, was a picture of the Sacred Heart, his arms outstretched, his eyes glassy and unseeing.

"I want to go home," I told him, in a whisper. "I'm not a naughty girl. Please let me go home. I'm not bothered about the holiday. I just want my mum and dad."

I wanted to run away, run, run, as far as I could. But I didn't know where they were keeping Freddie. And even if I found him, I had the problem that I didn't want him to see my hair. I knew he would laugh loud and long – or even worse, he would look at me in silent pity and shock. Ludicrous, that my haircut was the main obstacle in my escape plans. Problem one, was that I was stuck in a convent and not a holiday camp. Problem two, was that I'd had my hair cut off. That weighed as heavily on my mind as my whole predicament.

But I was just a little girl, and my hair was important. Either that, or maybe, subconsciously, I was using my hair, or lack of it, as a shield – as an excuse not to find Freddie. Because deep down, I think I knew, that this was no holiday and there was no way out.

Chapter Six

Some time later, probably around 7pm, a bell rang. It was an angry, urgent sound, clanging, nearer and nearer to my door. I poked my head out and saw a line of girls, all kneeling, all in prayer. There was one little girl outside the next door along, and she turned her head towards me.

"Get your rosary beads and kneel down," she hissed. "Be quick. She's coming."

I did as she said, and bowed my head, joining in with the chant of "Our Father" and then on, into a decade of the Rosary, my little fingers pressing each bead, holding on for dear life. Prayer after prayer, until my knees were numb and sore.

Sister Isobel prowled up and down the corridor, waiting – praying – to catch someone out.

When it was over, at last, there was a stampede for the bathrooms.

"Clean! Inside and out!" Sister Isobel demanded, examining our hands and faces as we filed past her inspection point.

And then, it was back to the dormitory. This time, the little girl who had knelt next to me followed me in and perched on the end of the spare, second bed. She was a little bigger than me, though still small. Perhaps around eight years old. She had blonde hair and a pale complexion and a soft, sweet, little face.

I found my clothes, under my bed, and for a moment I buried my face in them and breathed in the smell of home.

Then I hid them in-between the mattress and the bed springs. I would be needing them again soon. I was sure of it.

"What are you doing?" asked the girl. "You need to be quick, Sister Isobel will be round soon."

As she spoke, she stood up and walked to the door. She seemed to sense my anxiety, and she paused and smiled.

"You'll be OK," she said kindly. "Just get into bed and be quiet. Lie in your bed without crumpling your sheets and join your hands.

"Everyone has to do it. You'll get used to it."

Her smile faded as she pulled my door closed and went back to her own room. I couldn't work out why on earth she was being so nice to me. I couldn't believe there was any kindness at all in this monstrous place.

I tried to pull back my sheets, but they were as starched and hard as my night gown and getting into bed felt like climbing in-between two wooden boards. I was frozen, too, shivering with cold and fright. I was used to company, five or six in a bed, the warmth and comfort and safety of my brothers and sisters. All the times, at home, I had longed for a bed of my own suddenly flashed before me and I realised how stupid I had been. I had all the space in the world here. My own chair. My own bed. But I hated it. I was used to being squashed up and crammed in, being pushed about and sat upon.

I just wanted to go back to that.

The thought of Peter, Christine, Johnny and Jeanie, all snuggled up in the big bed together was too much for me to bear. For one stomach-turning moment it occurred to me that they would now have lots more room and be so much more comfortable, with me and Freddie gone. Was that why they had sent us here – to make room in the bed? After all, I *was* used to making way for the little ones, so perhaps this was the next, appalling sacrifice I would have to make.

But then, I remembered my dad's smile and his promise: "You're going on holiday." And I knew I could trust him. Of course I could. No, whatever had gone wrong, it was not my family's fault. And I had to hold on to that.

The tears rolled down my cheeks, quietly at first, but as my desperation took hold, I began to wail, loud, racking sobs that threatened to choke me.

I was crying so loudly, I didn't even hear my door opening.

"Don't keep crying. Don't make any noise. I can hear you down the corridor. You're going to get yourself in bother."

It was the little girl again. She whispered it kindly. She meant well, I knew. But I couldn't stop. I wouldn't stop.

My tears were all I had left. I buried my face in the pillow and wished that I was crammed in the bed back home with my family and the overwhelming stench of urine and belonging.

The little girl padded across to my bed and shook my arm.

"Sister Isobel will be round to check any minute now. Straighten up. She loses her rag if you mess up the sheets." And then, darkly, she added: "And make sure your eyes are closed, whatever you do."

I shuddered. I wasn't sure whether looking at Sister Isobel was forbidden because she was a saint. Or rather some sort of witch. If I kept my eyes open would I burst into flames – or turn into a toad?

"Eyes closed, eyes closed," I whispered fervently.

The ghostly little girl vanished as quietly and quickly as she had appeared.

Sure enough, not too long afterwards, I heard the clack clack of Sister Isobel and her pious, predatory shoes, advancing down the hallway. I heard the door swing open and, in spite of myself, I had to take a peep. My fear of being turned into a reptile was outweighed by a grim, childish curiosity.

Opening one eye just a tiny bit, I saw a ghostly figure, all in white, shining a lamp into the room. Rigid with fear, I huddled under the unwieldy sheet, perfectly still and straight, with my hands folded over the top, as if in prayer.

Chapter Six

"Are you asleep?" said a cold voice.

In the next moment she had vanished, gliding away like an apparition in the half-light. But she was back to haunt me, even in sleep.

After she had gone, I realised, quite bizarrely, that she had a shaved head, like me. It was the first time I had ever seen a nun without a veil and I wondered if they all had the same severe hairstyle. She had on a floor-length nightdress though, which added to my suspicions that she had crow's feet, and not human legs, underneath.

I wondered where she slept too – or even if she slept? I had ghoulish visions of her lowering herself, like a vampire, into a wooden coffin for the night. Or maybe she patrolled these corridors all night long, just waiting for a child to open one eye. Just waiting to smack those thin lips together and turn her victim into stone.

A shiver ran through me. I had never felt so scared.

With the room quiet once again, I could just about make out the picture of the Sacred Heart, dimly illuminated by a sliver of light from under the bedroom door.

"Nowt for your comfort here," he seemed to say, as I shivered in my starchy prison. "Nowt for your comfort here at all."

And though it was the Sacred Heart who spoke to me, he sounded just like my dad. He had a warm voice, always on the edge of a joke, and was broadly and unmistakably Northern.

"Where are you dad?" I whispered silently. "Why aren't you here yet?"

I waited and waited, and in-between my bouts of crying, I listened carefully for the determined footsteps and the raised voices I was so sure would be coming for me.

My mum and dad would definitely have had word by now that the holiday had gone horribly wrong. Dad would be on a bus, on his way to find me and take me home. He would not let me down.

"Hold the fort, Mairin," I heard him say, through the darkness. "I'll be there soon."

The hours passed and, apart from the giggling of the older girls further down the corridor, there was no sound.

"He will come," I told myself. "He will come for us."

* * *

Somehow, at some point, I must have drifted into an uneasy doze. Because at 6am, I was woken abruptly by the same loud, insistent bell from the night before. I made my bed quickly, smoothing out all the creases as I had been advised.

Out in the corridor, the little girl was already there, and I watched, bemused, as she dropped to her knees and began reciting the *Our Father* out loud. Then, I heard the clackety clack of Sister Isobel's shoes and I fell to my knees, grasping my rosary beads. Sister Isobel passed me without a word. I was only six, but I was catching on quick.

We trooped off to the washrooms where we washed and dried ourselves in silence. Under Sister Isobel's hawk-like stare, we walked single file down to a small room which was stacked with brushes and buckets.

"Take a bucket and a brush, little Kibby," said one of the big girls, her voice in my ear, so close I could feel her damp breath on my neck.

"Time to go to work."

We trailed back to the bathrooms, to fill our buckets with water. I was barely big enough to reach the sink, but the bigger girls filled the buckets and passed them back along the line. We were like an army regiment.

"No slopping," barked Sister Isobel.

When the bucket came to me, it was so heavy it almost wrenched my arms from their sockets. I made a half-sound of protest but the girl next to me gave me a warning glare and I thought better of it.

Out in the corridor, the girls got themselves into lines of four or five and began scrubbing at the wooden parquet flooring. I copied everyone else. My little fingers were soon red raw and stinging from the floors. Every now and again, I would catch a splinter in the end of my finger and wince in pain. But I knew better than to stop scrubbing. Already, I had seen Sister Isobel yank a girl up by her ear and drag her off down the corridor, because she had flopped back on her heels and taken a minute's rest.

When the bell rang, I followed the other children as we emptied our dirty water back down the sink, again passing the buckets down a long line. Then we replaced our buckets and dragged our weary bodies into the entrance hall. We hadn't even had breakfast, and already I felt exhausted.

Lining up in the dining room, we were each given a bowl in one hand and a cup in the other. One nun slopped a dollop of gristly looking porridge into my bowl. Another poured milk into my cup.

Swallowing my shame about my hair, I craned my neck and stood on tiptoe in the queue, desperate for a glimpse of Freddie. I was sure he was there, at the other side of the dining hall. But like me, he was painfully thin and small, and was lost amongst the crowd. I scanned the faces in desperation, but I couldn't see him.

Before we could eat, Sister Isobel said grace.

"For what we are about to receive, may The Lord make us truly thankful!" she announced.

"Amen," we muttered; craven, crazed in unison. "Amen."

By the time I was allowed to eat my porridge, it was cold and gluey. I managed a mouthful, because I was starving. And now that it was daylight, I felt a glimmer of hope, too. Maybe today they would realise their mistake, and I would be able to go home. Perhaps my dad was already on his way here, ready to scoop me up in his big arms and take me back to the poverty and deprivation I loved and missed.

Sister Isobel swept past me and I mustered up all my courage and said: "Will I be going home today?"

She spun around, fury flashed across her face, and she spat: "You have no home. You are a Child of God, Kibby."

"I am not Kibby," I stuttered, tears now streaming down my face and into my cold porridge. "When can I go home to my family?"

"You have no family and you are not going home!" she bellowed and all the other children jolted and jumped, as if they'd had electric shocks from their spoons.

"School!" shouted another nun, and the bowls and cups were hastily stacked at the end of a long table.

"It's the first day of the school year," Sister Isobel said, addressing the whole room now. "I expect good reports. Nothing but good reports."

I was totally baffled to be going off to a strange school. I had my own school, in Oldham, and the teacher would no doubt be wondering where I was. Why on earth were they sending me to school here? I was sure it was a huge mix up, but I did as they did. I knew I had no choice but to wait for my parents to come. Back in the washrooms, we rinsed our hands and faces. And then, I was aware of Sister Isobel, looming over me like a vulture, brandishing a small white cup.

"Drink this, child," she rapped, and shoved it under my nose.

Taking a gulp, I realised it was raw egg, mixed maybe with milk or water. To me, it tasted like congealed snot and I baulked as I tried to swallow it.

"You're malnourished," she said accusingly. "You need building up. We can't have weak children here."

And with that, she was gone. Still heaving, I rushed into a toilet. But the bigger girls were too quick for me and before I could shut the door, two of them squeezed in, alongside me.

"Nobody loves ya, Kibby," said the first girl, grinning with her wicked white teeth. "You're never going home. You're never going home."

I reared up, my little hands balled into fists, spit and raw egg drooling from my lips. They were much bigger than me. But I couldn't let that go. I felt I had to defend my family.

"My mum and dad will be here for me today," I yelled. "You'll see!"

I had shouted as loud as I could. But my voice sounded pitifully thin and was drowned out by the girls cackling and jeering.

"Poor Kibby," they sneered. "Ya never ever going home. Never ever."

I was filled with a rage. I wanted to pummel and punch them and claw out their eyes. But it was hopeless.

Their words rang in my ears as, robotically, I followed them from the washroom to a cloakroom, where everyone was putting on black shoes, kept in small individual cubby holes.

"Here, Kibby," said another of the big girls. "These are yours."

Chapter Six

I was handed a small pair of worn black shoes and I put them on. We walked in pairs along the corridors and out of the big doors, in total silence. I was used to wearing second and third hand clothing, but this felt different. I couldn't help wondering which little girl had worn the shoes before me – and what had happened to her. Had she arrived here believing she was on a holiday, too? And had she gone home now? Or had she met a grisly end? I shivered as I worried that I might be next.

We went down the steps outside the convent and my mind was racing with thoughts of planning an escape. But all around the grounds was a high wall, maybe 50 times bigger than me I reckoned, and there was no way I'd be able to get over that.

"Why did they need such a high wall?" I wondered. "Were we in prison? Was I a slave?"

I still wasn't entirely sure what a convent was, except that it was a place where nuns lived, and it certainly was not a holiday camp.

One thing was sure, there was no chance of escape this morning, walking in a disciplined line, two by two, with the watching nuns close behind.

We walked down a lane, past a row of neat houses, where there were women leaning in the doorways, exchanging sympathetic smiles and knowing glances.

"Oh, look at the kids from the convent, look at the orphans. Poor loves. Poor lambs."

Again, I thought about making a run for it. I wondered whether I should scream for help, and whether these women who felt so sorry for me would come to my rescue.

But the big girls were right behind me and I lost my nerve.

"Wait for dad," I told myself. "He's coming."

School was not far. A stone building with a smaller building at one side and a playground. We were soon separated into groups and I found myself inside a classroom, smelling of wood and chalk and looking and feeling just like my own classroom back home. It was strangely comforting and distressing in equal measure. I was given a desk, with an inkwell, and a book. I was glad to have something of my own that I recognised.

I was no longer on enemy soil.

The teacher wore a long skirt, a blouse with flowers on it, and a warm smile. Most importantly, she was just what she seemed, no more, no less; a teacher. And that to me was a tremendous relief. Because nothing, and no one, at the convent were as they seemed. I was learning to be frightened – of everything.

It was the first day of a new school year and so it was a new experience for many of the children. But in class, there was an invisible line between us and the others – marked out by regulation haircuts and shabby clothes that didn't fit.

We were the orphans.

Yet I wasn't an orphan, screamed a voice in my head. I had parents. My mum and dad loved me. Loved and *needed* me. I was the one, after all, who answered the door, changed the nappies, collected the wood for the fire. And I was determined not to forget that. That would keep me going until this mess was sorted out. Until.

The teacher had a big clock on her desk and she wound round the hands, trying to teach us all how to tell the time.

"So, with the big hand on three and the small hand on 12?" she asked.

She looked in my direction. But I shook my head. I couldn't concentrate. I could barely hear her voice. The only thought, stamped across my brain in big, urgent, letters, was: How To Get Home.

The day passed and afterwards, we were marched back to the convent, where our shoes had to be taken off immediately and polished. I noticed the other girls rubbing as hard as they could, as though their lives depended on it.

The nuns walked amongst us, checking our work, and the shoes which failed the test were thrown back at their owners for more polishing.

"You should be able to see your faces in these shoes!" rasped Sister Isobel.

But I wasn't sure I wanted to see my face, with my cropped hair and my sad, sad eyes.

* * *

Straight from the cloakroom, one of the big girls took my arm and led me back in the direction of Mother Superior's office. But to my surprise, we went into a room next to hers, where there was a man sitting at a desk. A nun I didn't recognise was standing at the side.

"I'm the doctor," he told me kindly. "I need you to take off your clothes."

Nervously, I undressed down to my vest and knickers.

"Oh yes," he said immediately, looking at my legs over the top of his spectacles. "Yes, rickets. Under-nourished. She needs food. This child needs food."

He scribbled something in his book and the nun said: "And the feet, doctor?"

He took a long look at my feet which, I supposed, were rather flat. I didn't know if that was lack of food, too.

"We'd need to operate on the feet," he said, shaking his head. "Let's see how she gets on, for now."

And with that, he turned back to his book. I dressed hurriedly and scurried back to join the others, feeling somehow that I had got away lightly.

It was that evening, in the dining hall, when I finally spotted Freddie, with the same confused, hurt expression he'd worn from the moment dad had told us we were going on that hateful 'holiday'.

I tried to catch his attention, as we ate, but it was impossible, with so many heads bobbing in between us, and so many sharp eyes watching our every move.

Tea was a kind of watery stew with bread, but I did my best to finish it, worrying that Sister Isobel might try to force-feed me another raw egg otherwise. Afterwards, as we filed out to the washrooms, I tried to hang back, to fall level with Freddie in his line.

"Marie," he muttered, and just to hear my name, spoken by a voice I loved, sent a ripple of warmth and familiarity through me.

"Freddie we have to get home," I whispered, urgently.

But to my dismay, he turned his head away, quickened his step, and soon the line of boys was leaving ours behind. I felt utterly deflated. I'd expected, somehow, that Freddie might have a plan. He might at least have asked me for mine.

"Freddie!" I tried again, in a loud whisper.

There were nuns bearing down on us. But it had seemed as though he had walked away from me on purpose, as though he didn't even want to hear what I had to say.

"Freddie," I whispered, a sense of utter desolation icing over me, like a frost.

It did not occur to me, then, that Freddie was terrified – even more so than me. And that he was most probably crippled with feelings of inadequacy and failure. What he could not bear to tell me, as my big brother, was that he could not help me.

I splashed my face in the washroom, the water mixing with my tears. And then there was Sister Isobel once again, threatening me with the raw egg in the cup.

"Drink it, child," she ordered.

And I had no choice but to glug it down, thinking to myself this must be what frog spawn tasted like.

That night, in bed, I sobbed and sobbed, wondering when my dad would come, and wondering how much more I could bear.

Through the darkness, I heard the soft padding of bare feet, and a warm hand took mine in hers.

"Don't cry," whispered the same little girl. "Please don't get so upset. You'll only make it worse for yourself. I can't keep coming in here every time I hear you cry. "You're going to get me in trouble as well."

I knew she was right. Already, I could hear the big girls screeching at me through the walls.

"Aw poor Kibby! Cry yer'sel to sleep. Go on. Nobody loves ya, do they?"

And, as my sobs grew louder, their jeers became angry.

"Shut up Kibby or we'll give yer something to cry for! Stop snivelling and go to sleep!"

But I could not sleep. The bed was too stiff, too cold, too lonely. And I was wide awake and ready, waiting for my dad to come and rescue me.

Chapter Seven

By morning, with the prayer bell clanging in the corridor, I had made up my mind. I would sort this out myself. Wasn't that what dad had always said to me, after all?

"Never stop asking questions," he would tell me. "Never stop wondering why."

And, I reminded myself, I was in charge back home, too. It was me who assumed control in times of crisis, and for a six-year-old, I did it very well.

"Hold the fort," dad would tell me.

I was his right hand man. I spoke to the cruelty man. I spoke to the social workers. And the policemen. So of course, I could speak to this nun and find my way out of this mess.

I could do it.

Filled with a false courage, I scrubbed the floors with a new enthusiasm, knowing this was to be my last morning here. By the time I got to the dining room, I was filled with such excitement, I barely touched my porridge.

When Sister Isobel came to inspect our table, she frowned at me, and for a moment I faltered. But then, with what I hoped was polite confidence, I asked: "When can I go home please?"

It seemed, at first, she might just ignore me completely, and so I said again, bolder now, almost defiant: "I want to go home!"

Sister Isobel stopped, quite suddenly, as though she had been slapped. She leaned over, her face so close to mine, that I could see an ugly long hair, sprouting out of her chin, almost touching my cheek. I recoiled in horror.

"You are never going home, Kibby." she hissed. "You have no home."

Something inside me snapped and I banged my spoon onto the table and pushed back my chair. There was a collective intake of breath as the room watched and waited.

"Get Kibby!" she said, her voice low and deadly.

She nodded at the group of older girls and I was quickly surrounded and marched out of the room, panic rising in my chest. On my way out, amongst the gaggle of gawping, goggle-eyed children, I spotted Freddie's face, pale and frightened and totally helpless.

"Freddie!" I pleaded.

He was my last hope. But he turned away, averting his eyes. I had thought I was a quick learner, but Freddie was obviously faster.

Now, outside the dining room, I was half-dragged, half-carried down the corridor and thrown onto a bed in a small room. Four or five girls took it in turns to hold me down whilst the others punched and scratched at me. I shouted and yelled and sobbed but even as I struggled, I knew it was pointless.

"Shut up crying, Kibby," said one of the girls. "You're giving us a headache."

Sister Isobel stood at the door and watched. But never raised her hand or her voice.

"Time for school," she said eventually, and I was yanked up off the bed and deposited in the cloakroom to put on my second-hand school shoes.

In the cloakroom, one of my attackers raised her hand to my face, and when I flinched she simply stroked my cheek gently and murmured: "Are you OK, little Kibby?"

I wasn't sure whether this was another torture tactic or a show of contrition. But to me, it just felt like another twisted form of abuse.

I didn't think for a moment that her concern might be genuine. Impossible for me to see it at the time, but she was just a child like I was. She was lost and broken, just like me.

* * *

My legs were so sore I could barely sit on my wooden school chair that day. Every time I sat on my hands, to try to cool my burning legs, the teacher told me off for fidgeting. I felt utterly miserable. And I was in shock, too. Despite all their troubles, my parents had never been violent towards me. I had never been beaten so brutally by anyone – until now. We had coped with desperate poverty and gnawing hunger without attacking one another. But now that I was here, in the very bosom of the church, I had been battered black and blue.

Back at the convent, I went through the ritual of shoe-cleaning and praying, eating and praying, sobbing and praying, all without speaking to anyone.

That night, after we left the dining room, the little girl slipped into my room, took my hand in hers and smiled. She had an exquisite face, so pale it could have been porcelain and, in my child's mind, I thought she must be a good person. She reminded me of a fairy-tale character and *Snow White* and *Rapunzel* were beautiful and pure of heart. And so I felt she must be the same.

"Don't cry," she said softly.

But I couldn't help it. The bell sounded for bed and the little girl left the room, but still I wept. Hot tears of frustration rolled down my cheeks and onto my starchy nightdress.

"Where's my dad?" I wept. "Why hasn't he come for me?"

The sound of my sobbing must have travelled because the big girls in the rooms nearby bawled: "Shut up Kibby and go to sleep!"

But I was far from sleep. My mind travelled back to the day we'd arrived here. I went through the events, over and over, trying to make sense of it all. Trying to see where it had all gone so horrifically wrong.

"Someone is coming for you," dad had told me, as we sat on the old couch at home.

And when the car arrived, it was him who had ushered us to the door – and out into the street. He had handed us over. Willingly. Without a word of complaint. Without a murmur of surprise.

"You're going on holiday," he had said.

The bile rose in my throat as the truth hit me in the face with full force. He had known all along. He must have.

I tried to push the thoughts out of my head. I turned instead to face the picture of the Sacred Heart, in the darkness, and I muttered a prayer. But a deep fissure had opened in my mind and the doubts and accusations were oozing in.

Did they send me away? Did they know about this?

Once we had arrived at the convent, it was clear we were expected. Sister Isobel was waiting for us. Mother Superior had plans for us. There were beds ready. There was supper waiting. Even at school, the teacher knew I was coming. She had a desk and an inkwell and a book for me.

It dawned on me, with a sickening thud, that everyone but me and Freddie had been in on the joke. Everyone had known, including my mum and dad. Especially my mum and dad.

* * *

The next day, I resolved to keep my head down and my mouth shut. I tried not to think beyond the moment. Tried to exist only inside my own head.

The rest of the week passed in a miserable blur, with my fingers bleeding and blistered from scrubbing the floor, and my heart bruised and broken from missing my home.

In every prayer, I whispered a silent plea for someone – anyone – to rescue me. At night, I would gaze at the picture of the Sacred Heart and my dad's voice would sound in my ears:

"You're a good girl, our Mairin."

That first Saturday, after supper, instead of going to bed we were allowed to go to the 'Reccy'. I had no idea what or where it was, but there was a buzz of anticipation amongst the other girls and, for the first time since arriving, I couldn't help feeling a little excited myself, too.

I stuck close to the big girls. The same ones who had teased me and battered me. For they were all I knew.

The Reccy turned out to be a large recreation room, with the same wooden floors and high ceilings as the rest of the building. There was a table-tennis table and a space to play and run around. There was even a gramophone, playing songs I recognised from home.

Best of all, there were no nuns looking down their long noses at us. It was enforced fun. Controlled fun. But it was the only fun I was going to get and so I jumped up, along with the other girls, and started to dance.

Chubby Checker was singing *The Twist*, and it was one of my favourites. Some of the girls skipped around in circles, others joined hands and spun around as fast as they dared on the polished floor.

"Let's spin Kibby," said one of the big girls. "She's the smallest."

I froze, frightened and wary of another attack. But then, suddenly, I saw this as a chance to gain popularity – and avoid more beatings.

"Yes, OK," I agreed, lying on the floor, offering up my arms and legs, like a sacrificial gift. Two of the girls picked me up and spun me around, before flinging me, like a rag doll, onto the floor, where I whizzed around madly. I acted the fool, arms and legs flailing, and it gave them a good giggle.

"Throw her again!" shouted the girls.

I was the entertainment. The clown. I was chucked across the floor like a throwaway toy, time after time. I exaggerated the moves, waving my arms and legs like an upside-down crab, trying to make everyone laugh.

Elvis came on the gramophone and I closed my eyes and imagined I was back home, dancing around the kitchen with little Johnny in my arms, mum singing along as she watched.

They threw me and spun me, time after time. My knees and elbows were grazed and it hurt after a while. But this was all about survival.

Odd, I know, that my way of avoiding injury was to be thrown onto the floor at full speed. I was taking a hiding now, to avoid a worse hiding later. But to a little girl, lost and far from home, it seemed like a good plan. And it was the only plan I had.

The next morning, at breakfast, the big girls were gossiping and giggling amongst themselves and I tagged along. I was one of the gang, I told myself proudly. Best of all, I was sure they'd leave me alone, from now on.

Sunday seemed to be one long day of prayer. After breakfast, it was time for Mass in the chapel, where the nuns fawned and fussed over a visiting priest as though he had just landed on a cloud straight from heaven.

"Of course, Father, whatever you think, Father, could I help you there, Father."

They were virtually curtseying and bowing to him – silly and overcome, like teenagers in a fan club.

It was all so confusing to me. Although my mum was religious we were not churchgoers and the chapel, hidden in the bowels of the convent, seemed a terrifying place. I struggled to remember to sit and stand and kneel at the right times and some of the prayers were unfamiliar, too.

Sister Isobel sat in the pew behind us and poked me sharply in the kidneys, through the gap in the bench, if I was a few seconds out of sync.

"I have my eye on you, Kibby," she hissed, quietly. "So watch out."

I had always believed that God was kind and forgiving, but in this hell-hole of a chapel, it seemed I had a lot to learn.

Perhaps I had enjoyed myself in the Reccy, or maybe I was simply grateful not to be beaten again, but for a few days I felt my spirits rising. I enjoyed going to school; I liked the morning walk and the classroom was an escape; a breath of fresh air from the stagnation at the convent. Each day, my hand shot up in class with a never-ending stream of questions; I was eager to learn and to impress.

And then one day, in the playground, as I watched the other children playing hopscotch, I met a little boy who, though he did not know it, was about to change my life.

It was a chilly and damp day, where the cold gets into your bones, and you feel you won't ever be warm again. I was wearing my grey jumble sale coat and wishing it could have been a bit thicker and warmer, wishing I could be one of these other kids, with mums and dads who kissed them each morning, tucked them into bed each night, made them hot meals, patched their clothes, and listened when they spoke.

In my daydream, I hardly noticed a little boy, about my age, sauntering towards me as though he owned the whole place.

"My big brother wants to go out with you," he said, matter-of-factly, nodding to the next playground where the bigger kids were playing football.

"He wants to be your boyfriend and he wants an answer."

I was stumped. How did he even know me? I didn't even have a name anymore.

"No, no, no," I stuttered. "I can't go out with anyone. I'm in the convent, you see."

I trailed off, ashamed even to say the word out loud.

But the boy just nodded as though that was no surprise to him, and he disappeared off to the next playground. A few minutes later, he was back, and he announced:

"My brother says he will wait for you.

"When he grows up, he is going to come and look for you, even," – and here he sucked in his breath superbly – and said: "Even if you are in Africa!"

With that, he was gone. I was dumb-founded. Where was Africa? And more to the point, why on earth would a little boy bother to look for me?

My own family didn't seem to want to look for me. So why him?

My mind was a whirl of questions. But as the bell rang for the end of playtime, I felt a fat tear rolling down my cheek, and I didn't know why.

This was the first time anyone had been kind to me for as long as I could remember. The little boy, whose name I didn't even know, had reached out to me in the depth of my darkness. And in the future, I would look back with so much gratitude and warmth.

Because at times of absolute anguish, it takes just a small token to restore faith and love again. I wrapped up the memory of that day and kept it safe in my heart. I would need it in the months and years ahead, more than I could ever know.

I never saw the little boy again. Certainly, were never spoke again.

But on the world map, on the classroom wall, I was astonished and secretly flattered to see that Africa was right on the other side of the world.

Clearly that little boy meant business.

* * *

And with one offer of friendship, I grew in confidence to look for more. And so, I plucked up my courage to speak to my one little friend at the convent; the little girl who had offered me comfort and help. She told me that her name was Dil.

"What sort of name is that?" I asked, screwing up my nose.

"Well, what sort of name is Kibby?" she replied, and I had to admit she had a point.

She got me wondering whether all the children at the convent had had their names stolen and their hair chopped off and their legs battered and beaten until they fell into line.

But I was too frightened to ask if that was what had happened to her. Too frightened of what she might reply.

"I hate it here," she told me, as we walked together to the dining room.

"Me too," I whispered. "Me too."

She couldn't suggest a solution though. She couldn't even offer any hope. But it eased my injured heart a little just to talk to her and know I wasn't alone.

It was another little boost.

And best of all, when Sister Isobel arrived at the washrooms with my snotty raw egg, I came up with a cunning plan. I pretended to drink the mixture from the cup, but then I realised that because of the angular edges of her veil, she had a blind spot to the side.

So when her head was inclined, I emptied the egg into the sink, quick as a flash, and it dissolved into the running water.

Sister Isobel seemed satisfied with the empty cup I handed to her, and I felt a quiet but overwhelming sense of victory. I was holding the fort. I was holding my own. And I wasn't beaten yet.

But the elation, if it was ever that, was temporary.

As we filed into breakfast one morning, I heard a commotion and saw one boy push another hard in the chest, so that he staggered backwards. And I realised the poor boy in the firing line was Freddie. My Freddie.

All sense of where I was swiftly vanished, and in a blaze of fury I ran over to the table, my blood bubbling with outrage.

"Leave my brother alone!" I screamed.

The boy was bigger than me, but I could still reach him. I saw the smirk on his face turn to something like amazement as I punched him hard, full on the nose, and blood spurted everywhere. My own fist stung as he began to yell and I cowered in alarm, my anger quickly displaced by fear.

"Kibby!" came a shrill voice behind me, and I swivelled to see Sister Isobel, her mouth set like a thin red pencil.

She nodded towards the same group of big girls and I felt my insides fall away. As I was dragged from the dining room, a bravado rose in me again, and I shouted: "Why? Why am I the one in trouble?

I was only sticking up for my big brother!"

I looked around, wildly, for Freddie and his support. But I could see him, shrinking back into the invisibility of the crowd, desperate not to be picked out.

"Freddie!" I screeched, as their grips tightened.

But it was no use. He had chosen his path and it was a different one to mine. I didn't regret what I'd done. I wasn't a violent child, or even an aggressive one. I certainly would never have dreamed of hitting a boy under usual circumstances, because I knew they could hit back harder. Especially big ones like him. But I had to stand up for Freddie. He was my family, my flesh and blood, and to me, that was everything. It was ingrained in me to fight for him, whether I wanted to or not.

Down the corridor, I yelled in panic and dread. Thrown into a small room I didn't recognise, I was pinned down on the bed, so tightly, it felt as though my arms and legs had been bound.

And then two of the girls began battering me with what felt like sticks. But when I opened my eyes, for a second, I saw they were hitting me with wooden coat hangers.

Curled up in a tight ball, I felt a wetness on my legs. I knew they had broken the skin and I was bleeding. And I knew also I had wet myself, through sheer terror.

I had no idea how or when it would end.

Through my pain, I heard Sister Isobel's voice: cold and clear.

"Leave her now, girls. Go to school."

I was still curled up, my eyes tightly closed, but I felt her lean over me, her rancid, holy breath on my face, and she hissed: "You will have to learn to behave yourself, Kibby.

"And I will see to it that you do."

Chapter Eight

There were times when I wished, I really wished, that I could keep quiet. I tried so hard to blend in as Freddie had done, almost biting down on my tongue to save me from more trouble.

But I found it impossible. Each morning, I would wrestle with my own, obstinate character. I knew it was foolish, fatal even, to speak out. Yet if I didn't, I might miss my only chance to go home. I worried they might forget I was there and keep me there for good. And if I made enough of a nuisance of myself, perhaps they would send me home out of sheer desperation?

More than anything, I felt I had to speak up, because it was the right thing to do. I was not an orphan. I was not Kibby. And I would not shut up until they agreed to listen. I remembered the little boy in the playground and his brother's vow to search for me, even if I was in Africa. Knowing he believed in me gave me a warm feeling.

"Somebody cares about me," I reminded myself. "Somebody likes me. Maybe now they will listen to me, because I have a friend."

I had noticed, too, that there were some children who came and went, without so much as a goodbye for the rest of us. There were tearful scenes in the entrance hall, little arms flung around bigger ones, cars crunching on the gravel outside. Their families had come for them. So why not mine? I had to keep trying. I had to keep asking the question. I couldn't give up. It was a compulsion, an instinct I couldn't ignore. Life-saving and life-threatening. But I had to do it.

One morning, as we scrubbed the same, hateful patch of flooring outside our room, I felt Sister Isobel towering over me. I couldn't say what possessed me, perhaps it was the Holy Spirit himself, because in the next minute I was on my feet and babbling – regretting it almost before the words had left my lips.

"Why am I here?" I asked. "I'm not an orphan. My family will be looking for me."

Sister Isobel's lip curled. The silence was horrendous. It felt like every arm and every scrubbing brush was paused, mid-air, on freeze frame.

"Get Kibby!" she snarled.

From somewhere behind me the bigger girls rushed forward, my nemeses with curly hair and pearly-white teeth, tumbling greedily on their prey and salivating with sheer delight.

I was wrenched up from the floor, tipping over my bucket of dirty water and screaming as I was carried down the corridor, away from my own room, away from the other children.

The tap-tap on the floor behind me was now as familiar as it was malevolent. The fear was horrible, almost worse than the actual beating to come. I was so scared, I could hardly breathe.

This was another strange room, again with one single bed, and no window. One way in and no way out.

I crouched on the bed as they pummelled me, raining down punches. Then with a paralysing dread, I saw them waving the wooden coat hangers over me. Each blow left me screaming and crying in pain.

"Stop crying, Kibby!" they shouted, their eyes lit up with ghoulish glee. "Shut up!"

And at the door was Sister Isobel, watching, impassively, her face almost void of animation. A hint of satisfaction maybe. Of a job well done. But that was all. Her lack of interest, the complete absence of emotion, seemed worse almost than if she had laughed and jeered. That bothered me more than the beating. It wasn't the violence that scared me. It was the passivity. The deadness in her face.

With a word from Sister Isobel the girls fled and I was left alone, stinging and sobbing in pain. When the footsteps had died away, I lifted myself up, gingerly, off the bed, and bent down to put on my shoes, which had been pulled off during the attack.

And, as I did so, I caught sight of a small, powder blue vanity case, under the bed. It was shabby and forgotten and only small, but it was the perfect size for me.

I pulled it out and for a moment, I forgot my tears and my bruises, and I smiled.

Checking the corridor outside quickly, I made sure that the coast was clear and then I hurried back to my room, as fast as my sore legs would allow, with the vanity case swinging at my side.

I knew I was late for breakfast, so I stuffed my old clothes from under my mattress into the case and hid it back under the springs once again. The bed was so hard and uncomfortable that I hardly thought I'd notice a case under the mattress.

Besides, it would give me immense satisfaction to know that my suitcase was packed and ready for when the time came to go home.

The bruises had not yet healed when, one night at supper, it started all over again. This time, it was because I hadn't cleaned my plate. Supper was usually my favourite meal of the day, just bread and butter and a cup of milk, but I always enjoyed it. But tonight, with the last attack fresh in my mind, I had no appetite.

"Eat up, Kibby," snapped Sister Isobel. "Eat up and be thankful."

"I don't want it," I replied. "And I'm sorry, but my name is not Kibby."

There were gasps around me, children both horrified and impressed at my impertinence. I tried desperately not to cry, not to give them the satisfaction, as the same girls grabbed me and carted me off for a beating. But it was no good. The tears flowed and my whole body throbbed as the punches started.

"Your name is Kibby," yelled the girls with a mad mirth. "And you are a child of God."

They spat it out like it was a death sentence, a terminal illness. I didn't want to be a child of God. I had my own family and I didn't need him. I clung to that, but I felt as though I was drowning, drowning…

Long after the attack had ended, I lay on the bed, my blood and my bones screaming out in protest and in pain.

I had left home thrilled that I was important enough for a car to come and collect me. Now, I mattered so little that I no longer even had a name.

* * *

I thought, as any child might, that I had reached rock bottom. That a broad brushstroke of misery had swept across my entire life and that the picture could get no darker.

But I was wrong.

We were in the dining room, where Sister Isobel's temper seemed to be at its most brittle, and I found myself on the wrong end of it once again.

After grace, we queued for our bread and butter and I must have been fidgeting a little, when her voice, crisp and cold, pierced me like a bullet from the other end of the room.

"Stand up straight, Kibby," she ordered. "God likes obedient and orderly children. Not rag and tag orphans like you."

The words were a sure and sore trigger. My temper flashed, my pride swelled, and I retorted: "I am not an orphan, Sister. Why do you keep calling me an orphan? Why?"

My feet left the floor as I was snatched out of the line of children and carted off down the corridor, into the tiny room and onto the bed. I heard a clatter of wooden coat-hangers and I braced myself for the onslaught which I knew would follow.

Sister Isobel stood at the door, over-seeing and all-seeing.

I cowered on the bed, face down, but the girls flipped me over and pinned my arms by my sides. I screamed as the first few blows hit my chest and legs. But then, to my horror, one of the girls lifted my skirt and began rubbing the coat-hanger against my knickers.

The blows stopped and the others ogled, transfixed, as though hypnotised by the horror.

Her hands went into my knickers and I retched, choking on my own vomit, but unable to lift my head. Time seemed to stand still. I felt like I was set in concrete. I felt like I was dead.

"Enough girls," Sister Isobel said quietly, more quietly than usual.

The girls fled and she walked over to the bed, menace in every step. I was no longer pinned down but I could not move. Every inch of me trembled. Every inch of me wept.

"You will learn never to ask why, ever again," she said sanctimoniously.

She might as well have been reading commandments from a stone tablet. She was so self-righteous and so horribly calm, as though this sort of thing happened every day.

And with that, she was gone.

The memory of the sexual abuse jabbed in and out of my mind and replayed over and over dozens of times a day. I found myself shaking my head, trying to knock it away, like a fat wasp. But it was there. Always. I didn't know what it was. But I knew it was bad.

Almost broken, I got through my days, longing for the peace and the escape of night-time. Only after Sister Isobel had completed her rounds, did I feel safe.

One night, as I lay awake, staring into the blackness, I felt myself lifting, slightly, from the bed and up into the air. I even felt the breeze up my legs, right to the small of my back, as the cold air sneaked up my nightdress. This was a miracle worthy of the Mother Superior herself. I floated down the corridors, past the statues, who smiled and winked conspiratorially as I passed. I carried on, out of the convent, over the high wall, down the lane, and past the school. I knew I was back in Oldham when I smelled the dirty chimneys and the rotting rubbish dumps, and I loved it.

And then, there I was. Back at home, with the old green front door, the moth-eaten couches, the welcoming Dickensian shabbiness of my home. And the big beds full of bony limbs and warm hearts. Just seeing the heads on the pillows, as familiar as my own, brought a big, painful lump to my throat. They slept soundly as I hovered above them and it was strange because although I was facing the ceiling, I was also looking down at the bed.

"Mum, it's me!" I called. "Here I am. It's your Mairin. I'm here to look after the babies. I've come home to help."

No reply.

"Dad! I'm back! I'm back to hold the fort!"

Nothing.

"Peter! How's your leg? Fancy a game of hide and seek?"

I was bawling now, shouting at the top of my voice, sure I could wake them. Sure, if they saw me, they would want me back. Why would they not want me back?

But they slept on. All of them. And nobody knew I was there.

"It's me!" I screamed desperately, my lungs burning and bursting in protest.

And then the hateful bell began to ring and Dil was in my room and shaking me by my shoulders.

"Come on, you need to get up!" she said urgently. "Sister Isobel will be round in a minute."

I grabbed my rosary beads and stumbled out, into the corridor, and onto my knees. But I had felt that cold air up my nightdress. I knew I had. And I had smelled the factory chimneys. I had been home, I knew I had. I missed it all so much. My family. My home. My poverty.

Chapter Eight

"*Hail Mary*, child, let me hear the *Hail Mary*," Sister Isobel demanded and I snapped back to my senses.

But already I longed for the next night. And the next journey home.

Chapter Nine

As the days became weeks, I saw less and less of Freddie. The girls and boys were so strictly segregated that I didn't even know where his bedroom was. And although I could some-times spot him at the other side of the dining room, he was rarely looking my way. And when he did, his face was pale and his expression was empty. He seemed to be constantly in shadow, as though the light could no longer find him.

I wasn't sure if he felt ashamed for not standing up for me, after I had stood up for him, in the dining room. But I didn't blame him one bit. If anything, it made me feel more protective, more concerned. Because I knew Freddie needed me, more than I needed him.

I was my dad's right-hand man, I reminded myself. I was used to holding the fort. And if I had to take a beating for Freddie, then that was OK.

As a little girl, I was so consumed with my own terrible situation, that it didn't occur to me that Freddie might be suffering just the same, too – that he wasn't so much ignoring me, as looking right through me; so traumatised, that he had totally forgotten how to wave and how to smile at his little sister.

Seeing someone bully him, right in front of me, was one thing. I knew how to react. But I couldn't – or wouldn't – think about what Freddie was going through every day. My own pain was all-consuming.

And maybe that was why Dil and I never really spoke honestly to one another either. We looked out for one another to a point, and we swapped snippets of banal conversation, sometimes. But I never once asked if she had a family, or why she was in the convent, or whether she would ever be able to go home. And besides, home and family had become such a distant, almost abstract, concept. I was unsure of myself, as though my memories, my beliefs, could no longer be relied upon.

If I was honest, I didn't want other people's problems. At six, I was already weighed down with enough of my own.

That said, I missed Freddie terribly. I felt as far away from him as I was from the rest of my family. But one Saturday night, we were all waiting outside the Reccy, while one of the nuns fiddled with the lock in the door. And Freddie suddenly burst through, out of the crowd.

He ran right over, and kissed me on the tip of my nose, before melting back into the chaos once again.

He didn't even speak and it was over in a flash. But I felt myself smiling, really smiling, all over my face. I had a tingle of happiness, down to the tips of my toes and back again.

Even as we walked into the Reccy, my nose was still a bit damp, and I giggled to myself, like I had a secret nobody else knew.

The big girls were all talking about the boys they fancied and the records they liked. They had a set of rollers in the Reccy and they would take it in turns to curl each other's hair.

The Twist came on the gramophone and I closed my eyes and let the music carry me away. Dancing across the floor, I was almost back in my living room, with my mum clapping along, and the little ones pulling at my skirt and copying my moves. Back to being a little girl again. A girl with a name.

And then, a hand shoved me hard in the back, so hard that I bit my tongue, and a cruel voice said: "Sit down, Kibby, you can't dance."

It was like someone had taken a pin and popped my happiness. I slunk to the side of the floor and wilted. The daydream was over. But the nightmare was just beginning.

"Ya think you can dance but ya can't Kibby," said one of the big girls harshly.

"Yeah, you're just a little orphan with no family and no name," added another, and she pushed one finger hard into my chest.

"You're nobody. You're stuck here for the rest of your life."

Each taunt cut deeper than the last.

"I am going home!" I insisted. "My dad will be coming for me."

And they all burst into peals of horrible laughter. Then it started, little slaps at first, across my face and my shoulders. But as they forced me into a quiet corner of the Reccy, the punches got harder and harder until I was cowering on the floor in a quivering heap.

I wanted to run away, back to my room, but we were stuck in there until Sister Isobel came to get us. And I knew if I tried to escape I'd be beaten even more.

Instead, I had to wait, and listen to the manic laughter of the girls around me. Goodness knows why, but I stuck to them like glue. It seemed the more they beat me, the more I clung on. I followed them round like a little stray dog, with nowhere else to go.

Eventually, Sister Isobel's voice rang out over the noise and everyone fell quiet and formed a line.

"Back to the cells," they muttered.

Yes, I thought. That was exactly what they were. Cells. Tiny rooms with no windows and no escape. We were being held here, against our will. Life sentences. With no parole.

That night, after Sister Isobel had completed her checks, I felt the silence settle around me, and I prepared myself for another trip home. I wasn't sure, even, if I could go at will. I just closed my eyes and wished myself away.

It was neither alarming nor surprising when I felt myself gently lifting out of the bed, and into the corridor. The journey back to Oldham was much faster than it had been even in the posh car we'd arrived in. But then, I reasoned, flying was bound to be quicker than driving. Over fields and rivers I floated; oh, how I hated the countryside now. I thought back to how excited I'd been, seeing cows and sheep from the roadside. Little had I known what a fool I was. How easily sucked in I had been.

As I got nearer to the house, I spotted a figure, walking down the middle of the street, pushing an old cart.

"Any old rags!" he shouted. "Bring out yer rags!"

"Dad!" I yelled, my legs paddling in thin air in my desperation to reach him. I had no idea what he was doing, collecting rags in the middle of the night, but I didn't care. Hovering over the cart, I looked down, my heart bursting with the knowledge that I would soon see my dad again. But as he looked up at me, my blood solidified, icy cold, in my veins.

It was dad's cart. Even dad's overalls. But in place of his nose was a crow's hooked beak, and the cold, mean, face belonged to Sister Isobel.

"You are a child of God!" she screeched, and she sounded like a bird of prey.

To my horror, dad flapped an enormous pair of black wings and there were feathers flying everywhere. I was blown sideways, rolling over and over, carried away from my dad, and away from the street.

When I opened my eyes, the bedroom door handle was moving, and I shrieked, imagining a giant crow was stalking towards me.

"Sshh," commanded an angry whisper.

The sound was far too harsh to be Dil. I had no idea who it was, and I lay, terrified, until the face of one of the big girls was right next to mine, in the darkness. I was flooded with relief.

But it was short-lived.

For in the next moment, she slipped silently under the bedsheets, alongside me. I stiffened, ready for a beating. But instead, she turned her lips to my ear and murmured: "Shall I show ya how to kiss a boy, Kibby? Do ya know how to French kiss? Eh?"

I was stumped.

"Do you mean how to kiss a boy in France?" I asked. "I've never been to France."

But she laughed a little and then her mouth was on mine, hard and wet, as though it was suckered on. And her tongue found mine, far too big for my small mouth, flicking and probing like a lizard's.

Revolted, I felt her hands, rough and forceful, under my nightdress.

"This is what boys do," she whispered.

I gagged and struggled against her, but she was much bigger and stronger than me.

It lasted only a few minutes but the trauma was seared onto the lining of my brain like I had been branded with a hot iron.

"Sshh," she ordered again.

And then she was gone. She had no need to warn me not to tell anyone. She didn't need to threaten or bribe or cajole me. Because after all, who on earth could I tell?

There was an imprint and a stench on my sheets, so strong and tangible, she may as well have shed a skin and left the shell behind. I lay there, gagging on the toxicity.

Again, I didn't know what this was. I didn't associate it with the sexual assaults from the weeks before. But I knew for certain that it was filthy and depraved and it left me feeling so wretched, so utterly desolate that I wished with all my heart not to wake up the next morning.

I tried hard to focus on the little boy in the playground. On his brother who would go to the ends of the earth to find me. But, like Africa, they both seemed so impossibly and unattainably far away.

The shame and the disgust scraped away at my insides, gnawing at my stomach. I wanted to wash myself, over and over. To drown myself in the big, deep baths in the washrooms. To be clean again.

In the Reccy that weekend, I gritted my teeth, papered on a smile and allowed the big girls to pick me up by my arms and legs and spin me around the floor.

They laughed and cackled while I wept and bled inside. I was befriending my abusers, appeasing my captors. Quite literally, I was sleeping with the enemy. It was Stockholm syndrome through the eyes of a six-year-old.

Chapter Nine

As baffling and completely bizarre to me now as it was then, I didn't understand I was a victim. And I certainly didn't see that they were victims, too.

All I could do was whiz around in the Reccy, faster and faster, until it all blurred out of focus.

* * *

From then on, every so often, one or sometimes two of them would crawl into bed beside me. I'd hear the ominous creak of a door and the sound of bare feet creeping down the corridor towards me. And my blood would freeze in my veins.

Not this. Anything, please, Our Lady, Mother of God. But not this.

"This is how to kiss a boy, Kibby," they whispered. "This is how to make a boy happy."

It was nonsense, I knew that. They were liars. I knew what made boys happy. And it was footballs and conkers. Catapults and sticks. Farts and Mud. Not this.

But there was a reptilian hand in my knickers and as the pain shot through me, a hand was clamped over my mouth to stifle my screams.

"We're training you up," hissed the girl. "Ready for the boys."

My own hand was forced under her nightdress too and I recoiled. She had reached puberty and her body and its strange parts were alien and hideous to me.

I had to get away. I couldn't bear it. My whole body was convulsing, retching, revolting. This wasn't what boys did. I knew what boys did.

And suddenly, there I was, climbing the steep hill near my home, puffing and out of breath, with Peter and Freddie, dragging our homemade bogey behind us.

"You're so clever, Freddie," I was saying. "Fancy building this all on your own."

And Freddie was shrugging his shoulders casually as if to say: "It was nothing really, no bother at all."

He'd found some old wood on a scrap heap behind our house and the bigger boys on the street had helped him fix on a pair of pram wheels. He'd stuck a cardboard box on top of the wood, tied on a length of string, and it was good to go.

It was to be my first trip in a go-kart and I couldn't wait.

"How do I stop Freddie?" I asked, spotting a sudden flaw.

"You just put your legs down," he said cheerfully. "Stick your feet out. You'll be fine."

We reached the top of the hill, pushed off, and I was whizzing back down, my long hair flying behind me, hanging on for dear life, with the wheels rattling and buckling and threatening to fly off.

"Whee!" I yelled.

I was thrilled and petrified, screaming and laughing, all at once.

There was no sign of me slowing down and so I stuck my feet out, as Freddie had instructed, but I was wearing an old pair of sandals and I skinned the backs of my heels. It stung like mad. But I didn't care. The bogey was in a worse state than I was, but we decided it would hold for one more trip, and Freddie and Peter jumped on together.

Watching them race down the hill, their faces a perfect mix of horror and joy, I felt my heart filling up with happiness. Yes, happiness.

That was what boys did, I told myself. Not this.

After it was over, and the girls had gone, the door opened again, tentatively this time. I knew, just from the sound, that it was Dil.

She whispered: "Don't cry, little Kibby. Don't cry."

But in my mind, I still was at the bottom of the hill in Oldham, carrying a broken wheel, and complaining about my sore feet all the way home.

My days in the convent were hellish. But now, at least, they became an escape from the wretched nights. I lay in bed, hour after hour, every inch of my skin prickling with fear.

"Please don't let them come," I whispered. "Please."

I felt like I was in purgatory, waiting for the gates of hell to open and drag me in. My ears straining; every nerve, every sinew on standby, I waited for them to come.

And through the deafening silence, I heard phantom footsteps, ghostly giggles, muffled voices whispering:

"Kibby! Kibby! Let me show you how it's done."

I couldn't work out whether or not they were real. The footsteps faded, the voices petered out, and I wondered whether I was going mad.

But even when the big girls didn't come, I couldn't bear to be alone with my thoughts. I hated being me.

"And who exactly is me, anyway?" I wondered.

Was my name really Marie? And did I actually have a family? I was starting to wonder whether it had all been a lovely dream, an elaborate story. The big bed in Oldham. The smelly tippler toilet in the yard. The poverty, the sweet poverty, and the sound of my parents arguing. Had I made it up, had I imagined it? Perhaps my name was Kibby and perhaps I was just another Child of God. I no longer knew. I was losing myself, piece by piece, as sure as if they were cutting off my fingers and toes and more bits of me, every day.

At this rate, there would soon be nothing left. And people would say: 'Who was she anyway?"

Chapter Ten

I had little sense of time and dates, but when Bonfire night came, I could smell the burning timber and see the smoke from neighbouring houses. A dreadful wave of home sickness sloshed over me.

Bonfire night had always been such an occasion back home. We'd go from door to door, proudly carrying an effigy built mostly from scraps from dad's cart, waiting for our neighbours to gasp with approval.

"Penny for the guy! Penny for the guy!"

Sometimes we got sweets or an apple. Other times a tuppence. Peter wore his leg brace, following his accident, and he was a great asset on the doorsteps. People would coo sympathetically and give him twice as much.

We went round scrap heaps and old warehouses, gathering bits of wood, broken doors, pallets and boxes. It was a competition, between streets and districts, to see who had the best collection. Our family, with so many kids, had a ready-made army of little warriors, out looking for wood. We won hands down every year.

"Proud of you, Mairin," dad would tell me, and I'd grow another couple of inches with the praise.

On the night itself, there was a big bonfire, on wasteland at the top of the street, and I'd get so close that my face hurt with the heat. It was a great time to be a kid. Just to be a kid.

But trapped inside the convent, the world outside seemed so far away, so distant, that I started to doubt whether it was still there. Were they having a bonfire without us, back on Second Avenue? Surely it would be cancelled this year. The thought of the world continuing as before, as though we had never existed, was almost too much to bear.

"Wait for us," I said to myself miserably. "We're coming home, Wait for us."

If I said it often enough, it was bound to come true.

I had learned, as a little girl, that Christmas was not about gifts and treats. There was no money for the myth of Santa in our house.

So I was curious and excited when we were all called into the Reccy at the convent, one Saturday afternoon, a few days before Christmas 1959.

"Santa's coming," Dil told me confidently. "Happens every year."

Sure enough, the door opened and there he was himself, a jolly fat fellow, in a red costume, walking down the wooden steps into the Reccy. He had one hand on the bannister to steady himself and the other was carrying an enormous sack of presents.

I looked up at him and clapped my hands to my mouth in absolute astonishment. I had only ever seen Santa on the TV or in books. Never up close and in the flesh.

"Is it him?" I exclaimed. "Really?"

At the bottom of the steps, he set down his sack, and began handing presents out, like manna from heaven. We clustered around, eyes popping.

Every child received a small wrapped gift. It was the first time I had ever received a present which was wrapped and, as I tore off the paper, I felt wildly excited. Seconds later, holding a pencil set and a drawing pad in my hands, I was over the moon.

As he left, Santa gave us all a big, Christmassy wave and I cheered and waved so hard, I thought my arm might fall off.

Later in the Reccy, as a Christmas treat, we were allowed to play musical chairs and musical statues. But I hid myself away and spent the whole night drawing and colouring.

They were all the same; pictures of a big house in a green field with a sun behind. I drew every member of my family, in a line, always outside the house, always where I could see them. No matter how many drawings I did, I never got fed up with recreating the same scene.

My plan was to keep them all safe, in the vanity case under my bed, until my parents came.

"When they see my drawings, they will have to take me home," I said to myself. They'll be so pleased. "I've got presents for the little ones. I've got something to give everyone."

It was as though I felt I could wheedle my way back into my home. The child's equivalent of sending money home from a job overseas. I felt like I was doing my bit.

I was still the right-hand man.

Every now and again, when it was dark and quiet, I would get the small blue case out from under my mattress and look through my belongings.

I had my old clothes, and my little grey coat, so that I'd have something to wear when I went home. Mum and dad wouldn't need to buy me a thing. I had my pencils – and my drawings, which I could share amongst the little ones.

In the Reccy, too, I had pinched a couple of crayons one day and they went into my case. And another time, I found a whistle on the floor, and I popped it straight in my case with the rest of my treasures.

They made a pathetic little heap on the floor. But to me, they shone like jewels. They were so precious; a secret route home.

* * *

One cold winter's day, I had just arrived home from school and my little hands were blue with cold. I was trying to rub them together, to get my fingers moving again, ready to polish my shoes, when Sister Isobel appeared at the cloakroom door.

"Kibby!" she said. "Come with me!"

It was unheard of to skip the shoe polishing and a chill ran through me. Doubtless I had done something dreadfully wrong and I was about to be severely punished. But there was no sign of the big girls, waiting to batter me and I was confused.

Sister Isobel marched through the corridors and I struggled to keep up. I had more sense than to ask where we were going. Anyway, I wasn't even sure I wanted to know.

We went down new corridors, that I hadn't even known existed. To my surprise, I heard the sound of babies crying – and one voice, above all the others, yelling and wailing loudly.

I followed her through a door and into a room which was lined with cots. I gasped. I'd had no idea there was a nursery, or even that there were children younger than me at the convent. And at the far end, struggling against a young nun who was trying to cradle him, was my baby brother, Johnny.

Forgetting I was in the convent and forgetting Sister Isobel was watching, I rushed towards him and threw my arms around him.

"Johnny!" I gasped. "It's me, my lovely boy!"

It was the same instinct that had made me run to protect Freddie in the dining room. Johnny was one of my own.

He turned his big, liquid eyes towards me and clasped his chubby hands around my neck. It had been him, making all the noise, throwing the mother of all tantrums.

Johnny was only three years old, but he recognised me immediately and settled himself comfortably on my knee.

I was overjoyed to see him; so pleased that I was lost in the moment. I took in big gulps of him, smelling his hair, stroking his cheek, kissing his fat little fingers. It was like a fix.

"My Johnny," I said softly. "My little brother."

Exhausted by his crying, Johnny soon drifted off to sleep in my arms. I would have liked to have cuddled him all day. But another nun took him from me and laid him in a cot.

"Sleep tight, little Johnny," I whispered.

But then, the horrible realisation hit me. Johnny was in the convent. Just like me.

"Don't keep him here," I pleaded. "Let him go home. Please."

But Sister Isobel was already frog-marching me out of the nursery and back down the corridor, her hand clamped tightly around my arm. I struggled against her, pleading with her to let me spend just a few more minutes with him.

"Not Johnny," I sobbed. "He's only a baby."

I couldn't work out what was going on. Were there more of us in there? And why? Back in my tiny cell, I sobbed and sobbed. I was desperate for news, but none came. I had no idea what had happened to my little brother. I didn't see Freddie either. It seemed as though our whole family was fragmenting and breaking up.

That night, I lay in bed with Johnny's screams ringing in my ears. Why was he here and what he had done wrong?

And as my memories unravelled, like a ball of knotted string, I remembered a night at home on Second Avenue. It was before Kathleen had been born, and I must have been about four years old. Mum was standing at the side of the bed, rocking baby Jeanie in her arms, whilst she sang an Irish rebel song to Freddie, Peter, Christine, Johnny, and me.

"Then since the colour we must wear

Is England's cruel red,

Sure Ireland's songs will ne'er forget

The blood that they have shed."

I loved listening to her sing, and I snuggled into the pillow with my arm around little Johnny. But as the verses went on, an anxiety crept into her voice. She sounded upset. Desperate almost. When the song finished, she started again, on a loop.

"Oh, Paddy dear, and did you hear

The news that's going round?

The shamrock is forbid by law

To grow on Irish ground!"

I didn't like the singing any more and I wished she would stop. It was disturbing. Little Jeanie was starting to grizzle and cry but mum just sang louder and louder. Then dad came into the room and said:

"That's enough now, let the children sleep. I'll take Jeanie."

And then mum did a very strange thing. The song stopped abruptly and she held Jeanie close to her face and began to scream – a piercing, heart-rending, horrible scream which froze my heart.

"Mum, please," I pleaded. "Don't scream at baby Jeanie. Stop!"

Dad took Jeanie in his arms and managed to pull mum out of the bedroom. There was a noise outside the door but then nothing. And we lay awake, in the darkness, unable to make sense of anything.

But now, as I lay in another bed, in another darkness, I wondered whether there was a connection between mum's screams and Johnny's screams.

I thought back to the way she had stood, silent and disengaged, in the kitchen, on the morning of my birthday. I remembered how she had knocked on Freddie's sore head after the car accident. And I trembled when I recalled how she had smashed windows and ornaments and had attacked my father.

Had she really meant to send us to the convent? Or had she been so ill, so unstable, that perhaps she had no choice. Had the social workers insisted that she gave us up – to save the rest of the family? I had always put my brothers and sisters before myself. Was this the ultimate sacrifice, for me to leave so that they could stay? Was this what was required of the right-hand man?

I had no way of knowing. But I knew, in my mind, that her screams, like Johnny's, had been a desperate cry for help. And nobody had come to save her.

Chapter Eleven

The idea of Johnny being kept – held – in the convent's nursery was very distressing for me. It was a lot for a little girl to carry around. It was too much. And so, one morning that same week, before breakfast, it all came tumbling out yet again.

"Sister Isobel, why is my brother in the nursery here?" I asked. "And why..?"

I didn't finish my sentence. The gang of big girls were on me like wildcats, scratching and grabbing me, dragging me out of the dining room and away.

The beating, when it came, was agonising. But it was nothing to the mental torture of not knowing what was happening to my little brother.

"Enough," snapped Sister Isobel and the girls were gone.

I scrambled up off the mattress, but to my dismay, she walked over to me and pushed me, by my shoulder, back onto the bed. There was nothing in her eyes to give away what was about to happen but I had a feeling of intense and nauseating dread.

Wordlessly, she took a coat-hanger from the cupboard at the side of the bed and held it above me, like an executioner. For a minute, everything seemed to stand still. Her tongue flicked across her lips, moistening them so that they looked like two slithers of bacon. Then, as if in slow-motion, the hanger moved through the air, towards me, and I braced myself for another beating.

Instead, Sister Isobel lifted my skirt and pushed my underwear aside. Inside my head, I was raging against it. I could see myself, pleading with her, begging her to stop – jumping up and down, pulling at the veil on her head, scratching her face until it bled, and spitting into her eyes of benevolent evil.

But in reality my mouth would not open. The words would not form. My limbs would not move.

"Come on, Marie," my inner self screamed. "Do something!"

I had been abandoned. By everyone. By myself.

After it was finished, she leaned over me and just for a moment, I had the horrible impression that she was going to kiss me. I knew I would not survive it if she did.

But instead, eerily, her cheek brushed against mine. The long wiry hair which sprouted from her chin touched my face. And then, she was gone.

It felt as though I lay there for hours, days even, stunned and sore. But outside of the chaos in my head, I heard footsteps and the sound of children talking. A little girl ran into the room and said:

Chapter Eleven

"Kibby! Sister Isobel sent me to find you. You've to come back to the dining room and have your breakfast."

I followed her, just because I had no strength and no purpose to do otherwise. I ate my porridge like a zombie and then I followed the others to school.

In class, the teacher handed out pieces of paper, and asked us to write a story, entitled: 'My day.'

"I'd like you to write about what you do before school and what happens after you leave here," she explained.

When she collected the work in, I had written nothing. Instead, I had drawn a picture, the same image as so many before, of my family, standing outside a house, with bright clean curtains at every window and a friendly yellow sunshine overhead.

I stared at it hard, before I handed it to her. I had to focus on them. I had to keep them alive. Or I would wither and die myself.

* * *

On certain Saturdays, I imagine about once a month, some of the children had visitors. They would disappear into the dining room for an hour or so and emerge, tear-stained but smiling, and carrying a new pair of shoes, or a jigsaw or a bag of sweets.

I was always so jealous.

There were even occasions when children went home to their families, for good. Sometimes, I'd see a little case packed, outside the dining room, and a child from our table, or one nearby, would vanish.

"She's gone home, lucky cow," the other kids would scowl. "Alright for some."

There were no allowances made, let alone celebrations, for anyone else's good fortune. Other children's happiness only served to accentuate our misery and we resented it deeply. My heart would burst with envy on those days when someone disappeared. I had an irrational hatred of those children who got to go home. It was as if every time one left, it made my leaving less likely. My odds lengthened with every occasion.

I was suspicious, too, of whether we were being told the truth. None of the children ever actually announced that they were going home. We didn't see any parents or grandparents coming either. There were of course no leaving parties, no ceremonies. We didn't even wave goodbye.

Could it be something far more sinister? Sometimes, I looked at Sister Isobel and I could almost see the blood dripping from her fangs. There was hatred engraved in every pore of her foul face. I couldn't believe that she would just allow children to leave, without a fuss or a fight.

But I was too frightened to ask her where they might be.

Occasionally, children were adopted into new families. Strange adults appeared and simply announced themselves as the new parents for a little girl or a little boy at the convent. The chosen child, half-terrified, half-euphoric, disappeared out of the convent, either to a better life or another kind of hell.

It had never been suggested to me that I might be adopted.

"Nobody would want you, Kibby," laughed the big girls on adoption days, as if the mere idea was hilarious to them.

I didn't want a new family, anyway. As much as I hated the convent, I wanted my family, not just any family.

But nobody, as yet, had ever even come to visit me. Apart from those five, wonderful minutes I'd spent with Johnny, I hadn't seen anyone at all from the outside. I couldn't understand it. Most of these children were orphans, so how did they get visitors and not me? I was the one with the family and the loving parents. Yet I didn't get so much as a letter.

It just didn't make sense.

But late one Saturday afternoon, when I was having tea, Sister Isobel shouted my name.

"You have a visitor," she announced.

I almost choked on my boiled egg in my shock. I pushed back my chair and stood up, but she shook her head slowly, savouring the control.

"No, Kibby, no," she said cruelly, skewering me with a single look. "Finish your egg and then you can go."

It seemed like all the saliva had been sucked out of my mouth and I struggled to swallow. I gazed helplessly at the egg in front me, and it looked like a large yellow and white mass, unfeasibly voluminous and unappealing.

How could I ever finish it? What if my visitor got sick of hanging about and went home? I didn't even know who it was.

Somehow, almost gagging, I managed to force down the final mouthful. Sister Isobel nodded, not in approval, but it was enough for me to be allowed to leave the table. I followed as she took me to a room near to the entrance hall.

As the door opened, I saw a celestial vision, and my breath caught in my throat.

"Mairin," smiled my dad, his eyes shining, running towards me.

He was carrying a little doll, under his arm, and he held her out to me.

"This is for you," he said.

I took her and threw myself at my father, my warm tears spurting so fast I could feel them falling onto my clothes.

"It's OK, it's OK," he soothed. "I'm here, Mairin."

"Can I come home?" I pleaded. "Please, Daddy, please."

He turned his sad face away from me.

"Not yet," he replied. "But you will. One day, you will."

It made no sense to me. Why couldn't I just go home, with him? Why was I there in the first place? Why me? Why Freddie? Why Johnny?

Weirdly, although I could not stop asking questions in the convent, I found myself unable to ask my father any of these things. I just nodded and accepted what he had said and stared very hard at my new doll until her plastic face blurred.

Chapter Eleven

Dad had always been proud of me for asking so many questions. But maybe, this time, I didn't want the answers. And maybe, this time, he didn't have them either.

"You're a good girl, Mairin," he told me.

I gulped back my tears and tried not to think about going home. I ran through a list of questions, safe ones that would not require difficult replies.

"How's mum? How's Peter's leg? Is my old dolly OK in the big bed?"

"All fine and well," dad replied. "All missing you."

But if they were missing me that much, why didn't they just have me back at home? And why would dad lie and say they were missing me – if they weren't?

My head swirled with the confusion, and I felt giddy and a bit sick as I clutched my new dolly close, buttoning and unbuttoning her dress and examining her painted mouth and her nylon eyelashes. Knowing she was mine gave me such a glad feeling, and it calmed me a little.

"She's so lovely," I said gratefully. "Thank you."

Dad put his arm around me, and we sat together in a comfortable silence, and it was enough just to have him near me. I wished it could last forever. But it was as though we were on fast-forward and the hour's visit we were allocated flew by. Before I knew it, I was being told to say goodbye.

And this was worse than anything before. I'd had a glimmer of home and hope, waved in my face, so close, so tantalising, and now it was being snatched back. It seemed too cruel. Seeing dad walk away was like having a limb ripped from its socket. I felt an unbearable, strangulating, sense of loss.

That night in bed, I clung to my new dolly. She had blonde hair and a fancy outfit with long knickers under her dress. I named her Winifred, just the same as my doll back at home.

She had a big pink smile painted on her face but, as I held her close, I cried and cried. I couldn't imagine smiling. Ever again.

The Monday after dad's visit, as we walked to school, I tried to imagine which steps he had taken on his journey. If I could fit my shoes into those same footsteps, would they eventually lead me home? Could I literally follow him back to Oldham?

It was a rainy day and there were lots of footsteps in the mud, across the grounds. But once we were outside the walls of the convent, we walked across tarmac and the prints disappeared.

I was losing him, losing him all over again.

I became frantic with panic and, leaving my place in the line, next to Dil, I threw myself down onto the ground and sobbed.

"Come on," she urged. "You'll get into trouble, come on."

Then I heard familiar voices, cackling above me, thoroughly enjoying my pain.

"Aw, poor little Kibby, her daddy didn't want her. Her daddy wouldn't take her home.

Chapter Eleven

"Nobody wants you Kibby! That's the truth!"

I wanted to be angry. I wanted to jump up and defend my dad and beat them all to a pulp. But I just didn't have the fight in me. I was in the mud, with my face in the dirt, and I felt I could sink no lower.

That night, after I had trudged wearily home from school, the big girls stole Winifred from my room and tossed her around amongst themselves, pulling her arms and legs and ripping her delicate clothes.

"Please don't," I begged. "Please."

But they didn't care. When they finally got fed up, and threw her to the floor, Winifred was still smiling stupidly. And though I wanted to protect her, I felt annoyed with her too, as though she was letting me down by smiling at the big girls.

Dad's visit, as much as I would not have missed it, was a hand grenade into my existence, and sent me into a spin. Once again, I began clutching and clawing at distant fantasies of Oldham. Now, suddenly, they seemed nearer, almost tangible. I began to think that going home might be a possibility, after all.

Chapter Twelve

On my way to school, each morning, I would gaze at the high wall around the convent and try to plot my escape. There was no way I could climb it. There were no holes and no gaps. I had checked, the best I could. The brick-work was smooth and even in most parts and I couldn't see a place for a foot-hole. The black wrought iron gates to the convent were kept closed and locked each evening. I was trapped.

"Think, think hard," I told myself.

But I could see no way out.

And if I made a run for freedom on my way to school, or back, the big girls would surely catch me and deliver a beating to rival all others. I dared not imagine Sister Isobel's nuclear wrath if I was caught running away.

Funnily enough, the easiest place for me to run away would probably have been from school. It would have been possible to slip away, in the playground, when the teacher's back was turned and hide somewhere until the search died down.

Chapter Twelve

But I never even thought of running away whilst I was at school. Perhaps because I was happy and occupied there. Or maybe because, like any child, I wouldn't have disobeyed my teacher. Or could it have been that my little friend, in the next playground, was counting on me? That I could not desert the one true friend I had.

And so, it went on. I grappled with two halves of myself. One part of me wanted to rebel and complain and ask as many questions as I could. I wanted to scale the high wall and if I failed, I had at least died trying. Another part of me, though, thought I should sit and wait, stay quiet and stay good. And my dad, my saviour and my hero, would eventually come.

I argued with myself, day after day, night after night, and drove myself half-mad.

One morning, at breakfast, there was a buzz amongst the bigger girls and I noticed the nuns were agitated and distracted. Sister Isobel was prowling from table to table rapping random children on the knuckles with a long cane.

"Get your hands off the tables!" she shrilled. "You are Children of God."

I did not want to be a Child of God but I sat on my hands, with a back so straight I could have had a rod in it, and I tried to avoid her gaze. I had the feeling she might turn me to stone.

It was not until I joined the queue for porridge and milk that I learned the cause of the chaos.

"A gang of the boys have run away," whispered the girl in front of me.

Instantly, I thought of Freddie and my heart plummeted and soared all at once. I wanted him to be free – but at what cost? And what about me, left behind?

"How old are they?" I asked.

"The big ones," she said. "Teenagers. They went over the wall in the middle of the night. The police are out looking.

"Sister Isobel will *crucify* them when they find them."

She said it with such relish, and I had a disturbing image of the poor boys hanging on the wooden cross, their swollen tongues lolling out of their dry, dead mouths, and I knew she was right.

I couldn't help feeling excited though; someone was making a dash for it. Someone was taking a stand.

"I hope they get away," I said passionately. "I hope they make it."

"Oh, they won't give up until they find them," muttered another girl. "They never do. Nobody ever gets away from here. Not for long."

I had never met the boys, but I felt almost patriotic in my support. I imagined them hiding in sheds, running through fields, sleeping in forests.

"Good luck to you," I whispered softly.

Even so, I wished it could have been me. A couple of days passed and there was no news. I lay in bed each night, in my starched and hostile bed, and wished more than anything that I was out in the wilderness, with the runaways. But on the third night, after our evening meal, a fuss erupted in the corridors and the girls began clambering on one another's shoulders and backs, to see out of the windows.

"It's the police!" they shouted. "The boys are back!"

I didn't see the police cars, but I saw the reflection of the flashing blue lights through the convent windows. My disappointment was swallowed up by my eagerness to catch sight of the boys as they made their return. We ventured as far as we dared, up the corridors, towards the entrance hall.

"Sister Isobel will be in the entrance hall, with the police," sniggered the bigger girls. "She won't catch us here. We're perfectly safe."

We were close enough to see a group of boys, bedraggled and cowed, heads hanging, as they waited. Sister Isobel was speaking with two police officers; stern, polite, reasoned.

"Thank you, officer," she was saying in a syrupy Irish lilt. "We do appreciate you bringing them back safely."

And then, as the big doors slammed, shutting out sanity and safety, she turned on the boys like the Grand High Witch that she was.

"You will regret the day you tried to run away from here," she hissed, the veneer of respectability slipping like a sheet of melting ice. "And you will regret it for the rest of your lives."

Nuns we didn't recognise were waiting to take the boys away, down a different corridor to a different hell, and then, they were gone. That night, huddled in bed, I fancied I could hear their howling screams.

Breakfast the next day, as usual, was humming with the next grisly piece of information.

"They have tied the boys to their beds so that they can't get away!" one girl said. "Fancy that! They were bound and gagged, and they had a nun standing guard over them all night."

I shook my head in disbelief. Surely not. It seemed too wicked, too macabre, even for the convent, to tie a child to a bed.

"It's true," another girl insisted. "And besides, those boys are not here for breakfast. Look around. They've vanished."

She was right. A ghoulish tremor ran through me. Perhaps the screams I had heard had not been so fantastical, after all.

* * *

My thoughts of running away had been brutally pulped after the boys' abortive attempt. I knew I couldn't risk being dragged back and tied to a bed in some form of barbaric retribution. Rumours were racing around the convent that the boys had not been seen since the police had brought them back. That the shame and notoriety they had brought to the convent, to the Catholic church and, above all, to Sister Isobel herself, was unforgiveable and punishable only by life imprisonment.

"Really?" I gasped. "She won't let them out ever again?"

Those stories, and that is hopefully all they were, struck terror into my very soul. I could not risk being padlocked away. I needed to be ready in case my dad came for me.

Besides, if those big strong boys could not outwit the police and the search parties, what chance did I have? A weak, defenceless, tiny little girl like me?

And so, instead, my escape plans had to be neatly folded and put away in the blue vanity case – along with everything else that was connected to my beloved home.

I had to make do, instead, with escaping from the convent, night after night, through the window in my mind.

I would float home again, in my starchy nightdress, and look down lovingly on the family I adored. I could not bring myself to call them dreams because they were so fiercely real. Some nights, I took Winifred along, and I was acutely aware that I was gripping her arm tightly, so as not to drop her as we flew along. Other nights, I could actually feel rain on my face and my bare feet were frozen. The funny thing was, although my hair had been cut so short in the convent, I could feel it flowing in the wind behind me, as I floated along. It was as if I had my old hair back again.

"It's me, mum," I shouted, when I got to Second Avenue. "Your Mairin!"

Sometimes, mum would rush out to greet me, her green eyes shining with excitement, her arms outstretched. Her face was young and pretty and vibrant. She seemed full of life, brimming with it.

"Come on Mairin!" she laughed. "Let's put a record on and we'll dance, just you and me. Just us two."

But there were other nights when she was so busy with the babies that I actually couldn't see her at all. She was buried under a heap of crying, crawling, snivelling little bodies. There were 10 babies, then 20, then more, multiplying with a disturbing and disgusting speed.

Mum was too busy to see me, even in my dreams.

And each escapade, or escape, or whatever it was, ended with the same rude bell, calling me back to my misery, back to morning prayers.

The days drained away, one by one, and there was no word from home. Not even a letter. And dull resignation set in once again and nudged into a flattening despair. The cycle of prayer and school and chores and misery – the huge, suffocating dollop of daily misery – continued.

I was no longer jealous of the children who had monthly visits from home. That little hint of happiness was a killer.

Chapter Thirteen

My seventh birthday, in July 1960, was allowed to pass like any other day. There was no announcement. Nothing. I was used to not receiving birthday presents and cards. At home, there had never been any money, not even for a cake. But my friends and my siblings had always wished me a Happy Birthday. My brothers and sisters would sing and pull my hair – one pull for every year. With so many siblings pulling my hair at once, birthdays could be a mixed blessing. I often went out of the room with a sore head.

But for one birthday, maybe my fourth, my Irish grand-mother, Annabelle Fitzsimons, had sent over a big box of clothes around my birthday.

"Look at these," my mother beamed, laying out the new socks and shoes, neat pairs of shorts and frilly little skirts, all across the living room.

We crowded around the box, taking it in turns to try on every item of clothing, never mind that it was meant for someone else. I tried on the baby's bonnet and Freddie put on my dress. We made the event last the whole day and we laughed about it for weeks afterwards.

"Remember the state of you in that dress," I'd say to Freddie, and we'd howl until our sides ached.

But now, in the convent, this was just another reminder – albeit a silent one – that *I Did Not Matter*. My identity, already blurred and confused, was being further eroded. I could trust no-one, confide in no-one. And so, I retreated further and further inside my own head.

I was so glad when my birthday was over. It was just another way of them grinding me down.

But soon after, in August, it was announced that, as part of a charitable project, a small group of girls would be travelling to Ireland to visit a convent there.

When my name was read out, I was both frightened and pleased. I had been so desperate to leave the convent – under any circumstances. But now that the moment was here, I found myself afraid and a little uncertain.

I was becoming reliant on the very thing that was ruining me. I could not be happy here. But could I ever be happy outside of here, either?

Not wanting to risk taking my vanity case, I left it safe under my bed. I put Winifred in there, too, knowing she might well get lost or stolen on the trip to Ireland.

"I'll be back, Winifred," I promised her.

I had never been out of the country before and to sail on a big boat, from Liverpool, was mind-blowing for me.

The big girls were on the trip too, and chased me round the deck, threatening to throw me over-board. I was glad at least that I had left Winifred behind or she would certainly have met her end in the sea.

"Nobody will miss a little scrap like you, Kibby!" they laughed. "Come here and we'll feed you to the fish!"

I believed every word they said and managed to hide away in an empty cabin until we reached Dublin. The convent, though I had no idea exactly where it was, seemed much like the one we had left.

Sister Isobel had of course made the trip with us and, like a degenerative, terminal, illness, I felt I would never ever be rid of her. She took charge and barked her orders as we prayed and ate and prayed some more.

The only difference was that I was spared any beatings in Ireland. That was a huge relief, but maybe not as much as you might think. I had got so used to the physical and sexual abuse that it was part of a very twisted routine.

Our short stay at the convent seemed, to me, to be spent almost entirely saying prayers. We spent so much time on our knees, it hardly seemed worth getting up again.

"You'd best pray we don't drown you on the way back to the convent," whispered one of the big girls in my ear.

On our return ferry, I was feeling sick and was desperate for the toilet, and a kind sailor showed me to the nearest one. But when I poked my head inside, there was no toilet paper, and I knew, from my stomach-ache, that I would need lots. I was too embarrassed to ask him for any, so instead I used the loo and hoped for the best. Afterwards, the big girls found me and began screeching in mock horror and disgust.

"Kibby stinks!" they shouted. "Don't sit near Kibby! She pongs!"

I was treated like an outcast. Nobody would come within ten feet of me. I was mortified. When we finally arrived back at the convent, Sister Isobel ordered me into the bathrooms.

"You're a disgrace, Kibby," she spat. "We take you away on holiday and this is how you repay us."

But even after I had washed and scrubbed myself, until my skin was raw, I could still smell the poo. It was like it had permeated my skin. I wondered whether I would ever feel clean again.

The smell must have been worse in my mind than in reality, because it did not keep the big girls away from me for long. Their night-time visits began again, with them slithering into my bedroom, and stealing away my innocence, before scurrying off into the night like vermin.

Their visits were so appalling that I would often be physically sick afterwards.

I had no idea where Sister Isobel slept. In fact, in my child's mind, I questioned still whether she ever slept at all. But I could not fathom how, under her watchful, regimented glare, such abuse could take place without her knowledge. When I later looked back, I would accept it was, in fact, taking place under her instruction. She was the high priestess, the cult leader, and everyone else had to follow.

One night, the big girls didn't come. And, as the minutes ticked by, and the door stayed closed, the dawning relief was almost joyous. And then, in the gloom, the door was opened cautiously and with a sense of relief, I saw a pale form, no more than a shadow, slip into the room. Dil climbed soundlessly and wordlessly into my bed.

I thought at first that she was cold and lonely, and I took her hand in mine. I was pleased to share a bed again too, just like I had at home. I patted her head, just as I would Jeanie or Johnny.

The warmth of her body next to mine was a comfort to me. But then, revolted and appalled, I felt her lips on mine and her fingers, like moist tentacles, under my nightie.

Not her, please, not her as well.

Blindsided, I gagged. All hope was gone. Stamped out and shattered.

She left my bed, closing my door gently as always, and Winifred fell with a clatter out of bed and onto the hard floor. I lay awake all night, my anger and confusion giving way to a smothering avalanche of pain.

* * *

Time seeped away in a humdrum routine of praying, scrubbing floors, going to school, and praying again. School was, at least, an escape from the nuns and a release from the gloom which seemed to hang over the whole place. As well as the normality, I loved the chance to play out, in the yard, with the other children. At the convent, we were not allowed outdoors at all, and I didn't understand why. All our play times, which seemed an exaggerated term in itself, were in the Reccy. And even the fun there was monitored and measured.

Each day, we had porridge for breakfast, a boiled egg or perhaps a stew for tea, and bread and butter for supper. Fish on Fridays. Mass on Sundays, holy days and whatever days Sister Isobel decided to throw in for added penance. The purgatorial beatings and the abuse, unbelievably, became part of that routine, too. They continued without any real pattern or progression. They didn't get worse. They certainly didn't get better.

Dil continued to creep into my room and into my bed at night, and though I was left sickened and enraged by what she did, I had an inexplicable feeling of sympathy for her, too. The abuse from Dil, or the root of it, was, in my mind, different. She was a sweet and placid little girl, searching for comfort and acceptance. And she could not express herself, any other way.

I think now that sexual abuse was all she knew. Much as I tried, I could not bring myself to hate her.

Oddly, too, though I never encouraged or reciprocated her advances, I did not fight against her, either. I never spoke to her about the abuse. There was no confrontation and no argument. It was as if, by never acknowledging it, I could almost pretend it wasn't happening. I didn't want her to have to face it, as much as I didn't want to face it myself.

And so, life for Dil and me continued pretty much as before. We would chat, superficially, on our way to and from the dining room and the Reccy. Though she moved rooms further down the corridor, she was always there, waiting for me, every morning. She covered for me if I forgot my rosary beads. She woke me up if I slept through the dreaded bell. But she also sexually abused me, night after night.

Though I was in denial about my own suffering, I worried terribly about Winifred.

"I won't let them do it to you," I promised her. "Nobody will touch you, Winifred. I will look after you."

She stared back at me with her unblinking blue eyes and her false smile. I remembered dad's visit, and how I had cried in his arms. And I longed to go home.

But there were days when I would wonder whether I had always been abused, and whether my memory of life back in Oldham was a false one. Or maybe this was what happened to all six-year-old children; perhaps abuse was part of the package, part of the pain of growing up.

There was nothing for me to compare my life to. And nobody, but Winifred, for me to speak to. Dil and I were polite to one another, but there was no real friendship there. There never could be. And I saw Freddie so rarely. If

I caught sight of him, in the Reccy, he was usually tearing around at a hundred miles an hour with a gang of other boys.

Occasionally, he would nod over in my direction, or he would say hello.

"Are you alright, Freddie?" I asked, and I asked him every time. I made sure of it.

He would nod and scamper off. But he never asked me if I was alright. I noticed that.

But there was never time to talk properly. I longed to talk to him. I missed him. Looking back, I think we must have manufactured much of that distance ourselves. Because neither of us could bear to verbalise our deepest fears, and the crushing possibility that we might never see our family again.

And so, like the abuse, it was white washed over.

Instead, I withdrew further into myself, knowing that relationships, of whatever sort, would only end in pain. All bonds existed only to be broken. As a means of survival, I had to keep myself very much to myself.

But late at night, when the intrusions had finished, I would allow myself a few moments of happiness, where, through my mind's eye, I would watch a reel of memories from home, greedily drinking in each moment, each feeling.

It didn't matter that they weren't all happy ones. They were home. And that was what counted. I watched Peter playing football in the street outside, limping behind the other kids with his leg brace, his eyes bright and his cheeks flushed with the cold.

Johnny was standing at the kitchen table, playing the drums with an overturned pan and a wooden spoon. Little Johnny, a lovable, chunky little boy with a mass of blonde curls. He had such a happy, placid nature and had rarely cried at home. But I shuddered as I remembered his tantrum in the convent nursery, arms and legs thrashing, his already plump face swollen with temper. What had they done to him to make him cry like that?

Then, there was fair-haired Jeanie and pretty Christine, snuggling up either side of Mum on the couch. Baby Kathleen, teething, was grizzling in her cot, her fist in her mouth. She had jet black hair and brilliant green eyes and she was a beautiful child; the very image of our mother.

Oh, how I missed them.

If I screwed up my eyes and concentrated hard, I could picture Mum brushing my hair and pulling it into a neat ponytail.

"There you go, Mairin," she'd say, giving me a playful tap with the hairbrush.

It wasn't often she had time to do my hair, she was usually busy with the babies and so it was left to me. But I loved it when she did it for me instead.

Another scene jumped into my mind, and this time I could hear mum singing her Irish lullabies:

'Too ra loo ra loo ra. Hush now don't you cry…'

And I could hear Peter giggling too, keeping us all awake in the big bed. Peter was the joker, always the one to make us laugh when we should have been asleep.

And then I saw Christine, sitting on my dad's lap in front of the fire, and I felt a familiar stab of jealousy. She and I had always competed to be dad's favourite. I had been the apple of his eye, his right-hand man, until Christine had come along when I was two years old. I was the eldest girl; she was second eldest. She had never been able to swallow that.

"I'm the prettiest," she would tell me. "I'm prettier than you, Marie."

It hurt more, because I knew she was right. She was a lovely looking child. But she made sure I knew about it, too, every chance she got. She'd admire herself every time we walked past a window. She spent ages doing her hair each morning.

There was a simmering rivalry between us, and we had competed in silly, child-like ways, for his affections. I was the one dad trusted to go out collecting firewood from the backs of the mills and factories near our home. But Christine was keen to get in on the act.

"Let me come," she had begged. "Let me help."

But peevishly, I had refused. Now, I would have given anything to go out scavenging with Christine at my side. I missed our bickering. I missed the insults. I missed everything.

Chapter Thirteen

Some nights, in panic, I would struggle to focus on their faces, to remember their features. My memories became woolly and distorted and sometimes mum's face looked too fat. Other times she didn't have the right dress on; the floral one, with the full, frilly, underskirt which showed underneath the hem. She had a long coat too, with big brown buttons on the front. As a toddler, I loved them because I thought they looked like chocolates and I had tried to pluck them off and eat them. But now, I struggled to remember the exact shade and texture.

I was losing touch.

"That's not right," I would tell Winifred anxiously. "That's not how she looks."

I had been away from home for over a year, and it was a long time for a little girl. I worried that I might forget them. Other times, I worried they weren't even real. In an effort to keep them sharp and alive, I would run through their names and ages as I lay in bed.

I would say them out loud, quietly, to Winifred. I knew I could trust her. She would not turn on me, as everyone else had. Freddie was inaccessible, but she was my one, definite link with home. I thought that by confiding in her she might remember them, better than I could.

"We're going home," I told Winifred firmly. "We're going home."

It was as if, by repeating it, I thought I could make it come true. I had to keep believing.

The Convent

Using Winifred's plastic fingers, I would count through the entire family: 'Dad, Mum, Freddie, Marie, Peter, Next hand please Winifred – Christine Johnny, Jeanie, Kathleen.'

I was desperate to remember. And I was even more desperate not to forget.

Chapter Fourteen

In December 1960, a few weeks before my second Christmas at the convent, it was announced, by the Mother Superior, that we would be taken into the town centre of St Helens, on a shopping trip, to choose a small Christmas gift for our families.

"A *small* Christmas gift," she emphasised.

But that didn't worry me at all. I was fizzing with the thought of the adventure. We each had a modest sum, donated by charity, to spend as we wished. It was stressed that we should be eternally grateful and thankful for this incredible slice of luck – after all, how else would scrappy little orphans like us do our Christmas shopping?

The donation was not enough, I was told, to buy presents for all my siblings and it would not be fair to choose just one. And so, I decided, after lots of thought, to buy a present for my mum. My hope was that, when she received the gift, she would remember me and come to take me home. This, I told myself, could be just what she needed.

"Would we be able to hand over the gifts in person?" asked one of the girls.

Again, my whole body was gripped with the excitement of it all. Could this really be happening?

But Mother Superior shook her head.

"The gifts will be posted," she said firmly. "There will be no visits to and from home."

My heart sank. My idle daydream of me knocking on our front door, carrying a present, wrapped in a big red bow, was shattered.

But there was still the trip to the shops to look forward to and, as always, I attached myself like a limpet to the bigger girls.

"I'm buying perfume for my mum," I boasted.

Perfume, in my opinion, was what posh ladies wore.

The shops were a blaze of colour and noise, with Christmas music playing and lights and decorations in the windows. There was a Christmas tree in the town centre and nearby was a local choir, singing carols, and I was fascinated at seeing their breath freeze and cloud in the cold December air. It was all so jolly and happy and there was a feeling of peace – it was everything that the convent was not. I felt as though I might be in a magical wonderland. St Helens town centre certainly felt much nearer to heaven than the convent ever did.

The perfume shop was mind-boggling, a mixture of beautiful smells and out-of-reach price tags. In the end, I settled for 'An Evening In Paris'. It was in a small, dark coloured bottle, the height of sophistication, and it smelled wonderful.

My mum, as far as I knew, had never had a bottle of perfume before and I knew she would love it. Better still, she would think of me and send for me, and perhaps I would be home by Christmas.

In my mind's eye, I could see our Christmas tree standing by the hearth, and Christine was busy making paper decorations and a cardboard star for the top. Maybe our Irish granny would visit, too, and bake mince pies and cakes and bring presents for us all.

"I can't wait," I said to myself. "I'll be home for Christmas."

The gifts were posted off, but we heard nothing more.

In Christmas week, we went to mass each day and there was a crib at the back of the chapel. I would usually have loved to stop and admire the baby Jesus and the shepherds and the kings. But I felt so uneasy in the dark chapel – as though even at Christmas I wasn't safe there – that I scurried out as soon as the last hymn was finished.

On Christmas Eve, Santa came, with more gifts from charities. I received a plastic child's bracelet which I loved, but quickly hid away, inside my vanity case, before the big girls could make fun of it and steal it.

That night, as I lay in bed, waiting for Christmas, I wondered whether Sister Isobel was in charge of Santa, and whether it was her who had summoned him to her convent. She seemed to me to be the boss of most people and most situations.

I was starting to think that she was even more important than God himself. Or that she certainly thought so.

* * *

The following morning, there was no sense of excitement or celebration. We had a Christmas lunch, but it was muted and measured, as was the way at the convent.

But over those few days, I was at least given a brief respite from the attacks.

At the time, I saw it as a little bit like a Christmas gift, as though Sister Isobel, unlikely as it seemed, had been dusted with a layer of Christmas magic and she had called a stop to the beatings and the sexual abuse. Perhaps, in what was the season of goodwill to all men, she could not bear to see me suffer?

Looking back now, I think it far more likely that the attacks were paused because she was busy trying impress a continuous stream of Christmas visitors to the convent — and she could not risk being unmasked for the monster that she was while they were there.

Yes, looking back now, it was all about her, and not about me at all.

And so, she had to be content with simply frightening me with her withering looks and piercing glares, while charity workers and social workers, the local mayor and a bunch of meaty-faced councillors, all milled around the building, patting themselves and Sister Isobel on the back, for a job well done looking after the poor orphans.

As a mark of gratitude, we were made to perform a nativity play for the visiting dignitaries.

"You can be an angel, Kibby," said Sister Isobel. "You're one of the smallest."

"Aah, little Kibby, an angel," cooed the big girls. "Lovely. An orphan angel."

I didn't want to be an angel. Not at all. I thought back to the nativity plays we had performed at home, for my parents. I was director, producer and often the only one with a speaking part. I hated the idea of being a lowly angel for Sister Isobel.

Our plays at home had been full of fun and good will. They had cost nothing but meant everything to us.

I wanted to be Mary, on the donkey, holding the baby. But I was way down the pecking order and there was no chance of that.

"You can't hold the baby Jesus, Kibby!" scoffed the big girls.

At home, I was used to looking after real-life babies. Here, they didn't even trust me to hold a baby doll. Well, I decided, I didn't want to be Mary, anyway. I didn't want anything to do with their stupid plays and their façade of festive cheer. It was all a big lie to cover up the horror of what was really going on here every day.

I was handed a costume, and we rehearsed some Christmas carols: *Silent Night*, *Away in a Manger* and *We Three*

Kings. The older girls taught us the words, though I knew the first verses from school and from singing at home with my parents.

My favourite was *Silent Night,* because it reminded me most of home. For a few moments, as I was singing, I could forget where I was and it was as though a bit of Christmas sparkle was shining through the gloom.

Every time I lost concentration, or I got the words wrong, Sister Isobel would pinch my arm hard and spit instructions down my ear.

When the big day came, and the special guests arrived, it was as though someone had sprinkled fairy dust on the convent. The other nuns were cheery and friendly. Sister Isobel did not smile. I don't think her mean mouth could have stretched to that unfamiliar shape. But she was polite to the guests and she did not shout at us and that was as much as could be asked of her. The play was performed in a different building within the grounds of the convent. There was a stage inside, and rows of chairs set out.

I would have loved it, had it not been that Sister Isobel's face, staring back at us from the audience, was set in a sort of smiley grimace and it was very off-putting. When our performance was finished, she clapped but her face was strained with the effort.

I could not work the sudden change out at all.

"She's trying to impress the priest, Kibby," one of the big girls told me. "You're so stupid."

So that was it. I wondered whether Sister Isobel and the priest were getting married and perhaps she didn't want to put him off with her sour temperament. And as soon as the important visitors had gone, she was back to her old self.

"Prayers, girls!" she ordered sharply. "And we will say an extra decade of the Rosary to mark the festive period."

But in any case, she must have made a good impression – we all must. Because soon after, it was announced that a man from the hospital, a man inside an iron lung, no less, would be our next visitor. He was coming to the convent so that we could pray for him.

"You are children of God!" thundered Sister Isobel. "You must pray for this poor man. Pray that the Lord will help him."

I had no idea what an iron lung was, but a few days later the contraption arrived, looking like a submarine. It was wheeled into the middle of the Reccy, and we were all instructed to gather around, form a circle, and pray. But as we finished our first decade of the Rosary, my curiosity overcame me, and I knocked, gently, on the casing.

"Are you alright in there?" I asked. "Can you hear me?"

"Yes I can!" replied a weak voice.

There was a ripple of laughter amongst the other kids before Sister Isobel hooked me, like a gasping fish, and pulled me out of the circle.

"Kibby!" she said coldly. "Always you. Always. Stop asking questions!"

She threw me into one of the torture rooms and I waited, knowing what was coming next, but powerless to stop it. I saw the wooden coat hangers, as they crashed down upon me, and I yelled in agony. I had no idea what was wrong with the poor bloke inside the iron lung, but I knew with total certainty that I would rather have been in his shoes than mine.

I didn't even understand what I had done wrong. I had only wanted to check on him. I felt sorry for him, that he could not clamber out and dance with us in the Reccy or have a game of hide and seek. I wondered if he liked Chubby Checker, or Elvis, or Helen Shapiro.

But I knew better than to open my mouth again.

The next week, he was wheeled in once again, like a pilgrim in a rocket, and we clustered around him, excited by the small break in our routine.

I began to look forward to the visits from the man in the iron lung. I saved my questions up and tried them on Winifred instead, at night.

"So why is he in there, Winifred?" I asked. "And will he ever get better? And has he been taken away from his family, too?"

I even toyed with the idea of enlisting him as a partner in crime; could I in some way pass a message through him, to the nurses at the hospital, and then on to my parents?

But one week, he did not come. We heard nothing more of the man in the iron lung. And sadly, I wondered whether our prayers had not worked as well as we had hoped.

Chapter Fourteen

* * *

I was growing up fast and learning, as much as I could, to keep quiet. All curiosity, all imagination, had been snuffed out and crucified by Sister Isobel and her hench-girls.

But there were times when, peculiarly, I got into trouble for saying nothing at all. It felt as though I just could not win.

One day, I had just finished eating my boiled egg in the dining room when Sister Isobel came over and picked up the empty shell in disgust.

"You ungrateful, deceitful child!" she seethed. "You have deliberately wasted food, when millions in the world are starving to death!"

I stared, totally perplexed. I had finished the egg. I knew I had.

Then, she took a knife and scraped out the thinnest sliver of egg white, almost the first layer of the shell, and rammed it between my lips.

"Never leave food!" she menaced and with that, she beckoned to the big girls who were waiting for her signal.

Again, even as the punches rained down, I had no idea what my mistake had been. They beat me so hard that for days I could not bear to sit or lie down, without biting back tears. I cuddled Winifred, late at night, and together again we ran through the list of my family members. It was a lifeline and I clung to it, though I felt at times I was sinking fast.

Even at school, the teacher raised an eyebrow when she saw the black and purple map across my arms and legs. Usually my bruises were covered by my clothes, but this time, the girls had been careless. They had enjoyed themselves too much and got carried away.

"How did this happen?" asked my teacher.

But I shook my head.

When there was an opportunity for me to speak up, I found that I couldn't. Sister Isobel had made sure of that.

Chapter Fifteen

On Ash Wednesday, in February 1961, there was a special service in the chapel to mark the start of Lent. Once again, Sister Isobel fussed over the priest as though he was the pope himself.

"This is the start of Lent," she told us viciously. "Forty days and forty nights of suffering. And it was all for you.

"You are all sinners, children, every one of you."

I shifted uncomfortably. I had such bad thoughts about Sister Isobel. I noticed she had not included herself in the list of sinners. I noticed that *she* was showing no gratitude and no humility. But I felt uneasy, as she preached, I feared that she could read my mind and she was speaking directly to me.

This God was completely different to the one I'd prayed to back at home. The God my mother knew was the one who fixed broken limbs and heads, sent food when there was none in the cupboard, and let us off when we were naughty. But the God here was a tyrant and a bully, ordering his wife, Sister Isobel, (or was she married to the priest?) to beat and torture us and make us cry.

At the end of the *Our Father*, we would all chant "And deliver us from evil."

It made no sense at all to me. Deliver us from evil? Surely, we were stuck in the very middle of it. To a seven-year-old, it was very confusing.

After Mass had ended, we all paraded around with black ash marks on our foreheads, too terrified to wash in case they wore off and we burned in hell. To me, they were also a sign that I was one of the gang. And I liked that. I was desperate to belong somewhere – anywhere.

Sister Isobel seemed to relish the period of Lent, as a chance to make our lives more miserable than ever. We didn't actually give anything up as other children often do, because, of course, there was nothing left to take away from our lives. We had no sweets, no treats, nothing to look forward to anyway.

All the nuns took Lent very seriously, and the atmosphere in the convent became even more repressed and stifled than usual. All the statues and holy pictures were covered with purple cloths which added to the feeling of gloom. And it frightened me, too. Why were the statues covered? What did the nuns want them not to see?

I began to worry that they were planning some kind of mass punishment – the worst yet – and that the statues were not allowed to see it. I had never actually seen any other children being punished, but then, there were never any witnesses to my beatings either, except for the big girls who were taking part. Sister Isobel always made sure I was in a quiet room, away from prying eyes.

Perhaps in Lent, there was going to be a wide-scale attack. A religious onslaught. The idea made me even more anxious than usual.

Sister Isobel seemed to thrive on the Lenten misery and we were assigned more tasks, more scrubbing, more praying, than before. Whenever there was free time, she would bark, "Buckets and brushes, girls!" and we would have to get down on our hands and knees and scrub every inch of every floor. When they were finished, there were windows to wash.

The place was clinically, carbolically, clean. The smell of soap stung the insides of my nostrils. It was so clean, it was unhealthy.

And though we were cleaning and scrubbing to the point of collapse, she rationed our food, too. Some nights, there was no supper at all.

"He starved for you!" she said accusingly, her eyes boring into mine, as though it was all my fault.

I didn't see how starving me would help Jesus in any way and I opened my mouth to say so.

"But why?"

And that was as far as I got before the bigger girls pounced on me and the usual assaults began.

"You never learn, Kibby," laughed one of the girls in delight.

But it wasn't that I didn't learn. More that I didn't want to. They had stolen away everything I had – but I was determined they wouldn't break my spirit. Not yet, at any rate.

My questions were all I had left.

At the start of Easter week, the largest Easter Egg I had ever seen suddenly appeared in the dining room, as if by magic.

Word went round that it had been donated to the convent, by a charity, and that it was a gift for the orphans. Just looking at it made me lick my lips. I had never had an Easter Egg in my life, never even seen one so close up, and this one was magnificent.

I couldn't wait for Easter Sunday.

But the night before, in the Reccy, one of the big girls said to me:

"You do know the Easter egg got smashed, don't you, Kibby? It had to be swept up and thrown away. You can never have any now."

She and the other girls laughed as my eyes brimmed with tears. I had been so looking forward to tasting the chocolate. But it upset me more that the lovely egg had been chucked in the bin, without ever being appreciated. It seemed like a crime.

It wasn't until Easter Sunday morning, when I went back to the dining hall, that I saw the egg was perfectly intact. The girls had been telling me lies.

"April Fool, Kibby," they chortled.

It wasn't funny to me. But it was a relief to know the egg was in one piece, and I was annoyed at myself for falling for their prank.

Easter Sunday came and went and I wasn't given a single piece of chocolate. The next day, the egg had vanished for real, and I had no idea where it had gone. With my bruises still smarting from my last beating, I decided not to bother asking.

* * *

In the weeks afterwards, it was announced that I, along with some of the other younger ones, would begin the Sacramental Programme. In the afternoons, after school, we started studying for our First Confession. We chanted the prayers like obedient little robots.

"Bless me Father for I have sinned. "I am heartily sorry I have sinned against you. And by the help of your grace, I will not sin again."

But when the time came for me to sit inside the confessional, just knowing the priest was at the other side of the purple curtain was enough to terrify me. If he was indeed married to Sister Isobel, as I feared, he would likely be a very angry man and I was worried about saying the wrong thing.

And so, in my panic, I said nothing at all. When he asked for a list of my sins, my mind was a complete blank. I couldn't even make any up; I was struck dumb with terror.

There was a crucifix hanging inside the confessional, and seeing poor Jesus dead on the cross just made me even more flustered.

"Oh, erm, erm…" I stuttered.

The priest must have got fed up with waiting because, eventually, he gave me absolution regardless and sent me on my way.

Next came Holy Communion. This was the big one, even I knew that.

"The communion host is Jesus, so don't chew the host," the big girls told me.

"If you bite the host you will be biting into Jesus. Think of that, Kibby."

The idea that I might be responsible for injuring Jesus himself was troubling. But I was soon caught up in the preparations for the day itself.

One afternoon, one of the nuns took me into a room with a huge wardrobe and inside was a row of beautiful white communion dresses. I gasped, over-awed. I desperately wanted to look at them all and pick one out for myself, but I was not allowed.

Instead, the nun picked out a long white dress, with frills around the bodice and a sash at the waist. It had a full skirt, much like a princess might wear. When I tried it on, I thought my heart might burst with happiness.

I wanted to parade up and down the corridors, to show off to my mum and my sisters and my friends back home in Oldham.

If only they could see me now!

Instead, I had to be content with telling Winifred all about it, in bed that night.

"Wait till you see me in my dress," I told her. "I look posh, posh just like you!"

On the morning of my first Communion, the big girls took me to the Reccy to curl my hair. Still short, it was just about long enough to twist into tiny screw curls.

"You're marrying Jesus today," they told me. "You need to look your best."

I didn't really want to be married to the same man as Sister Isobel but I said nothing. I was so enthralled by the whole occasion that I didn't want a little thing like that worry me. Even when the big girls pulled my hair too hard on purpose, I refused to cry.

The nuns zipped up my dress and fixed a long veil on my hair, and then came the most wonderful moment of all, when they handed me a small bouquet of flowers. I'd never had my very own bunch of flowers before and I was euphoric. I kept thinking how lovely it would have been if mum and dad could have seen me, how proud they would have felt. I missed them being there so much! But I pushed those thoughts to the back of my mind when I was next handed a dainty pair of white Cinderella slippers.

"They're lovely," I gasped.

One of the nuns slipped my rosary beads over my head and around my neck. I felt like a beautiful bride. So, I realised, I was getting married, after all. I couldn't wait.

"You're ready, now," the nun smiled. "And don't you look a picture."

Outside the chapel, all of the nuns were joyous. Even Sister Isobel attempted a sort of toothy sneer which was her attempt at showing approval.

"This is the most important day of your lives," she told us, but she couldn't resist giving me a sharp poke in the back as I walked past, carrying my flowers.

"Keep your shoulders straight, Kibby," she scowled.

In the church, I spotted Freddie, sitting on the other side of the pew, wearing a large sash and a smart shirt and shorts. His shoes were shining and so was his face.

He looked shy and a little overwhelmed, but almost happy.

As we lined up for Holy Communion, hands clasped, heads bowed, deep in reverential silence, I began to worry again about eating the host. My mouth was terribly dry. I wasn't sure I could swallow it whole. And by the time it was my turn, I was absolutely certain I couldn't do it.

"Body of Christ," said the priest, holding the round host high above me, like a small moon-like trophy.

"Amen," I whimpered.

With my mouth crammed with what I was sure was the body of Our Lord, I returned to my pew and hoped it might somehow magically dissolve if I prayed hard enough. But there was no divine intervention and, as we stood to say the *Our Father* I knew I had to act fast. If Sister Isobel caught me mumbling during the prayer, she would have me severely punished, I knew that.

I had no option but to bite the host hard, and swallow. But the realisation that I had just chewed Jesus to death was devastating. I had to fight back the tears during the final hymn and the procession out of the chapel. I ran off to my room and threw myself onto the bed, holding Winifred close as I cried.

It wasn't long before a couple of the other girls, both in communion dresses, burst into the room.

"You need to come back for the photos," they gasped. "Your Freddie is waiting. Sister Isobel is going spare! Come on, Kib!"

Easily distracted as seven-year-olds are, I skipped off, ready to have my photo taken, hardly able to believe that the moment was going to be captured, for all eternity. Freddie and I had once had a photo done when we were babies, but I didn't remember the occasion. This was truly special.

"We can keep this photo forever," I told Freddie, as we blinked at the photographer's flash gun.

I could not bring myself to say what I was thinking:

"And when our parents see it, they will remember who we are."

I did not want to bring him, and me, crashing down, with talk of home. Sometimes, when you are so elated, as I was that day, utter desolation is just a moment away. It is nearer than ever. And I dared not risk it.

But I hoped Freddie was thinking the same thing.

"The photo will be posted home to your parents," Sister Isobel announced. "You are Children of God. They will know that now."

It was a huge disappointment that we were not at least allowed to see the photograph first. And sadly, I was made to hand my communion dress back too, and it was returned to the wardrobe, ready for the next little orphan to wear. It broke my heart to part with it.

Later, we gathered for night prayers and it was such a comfort to me that no announcement was made about me eating Jesus to death.

He had obviously made a miraculous escape.

Chapter Sixteen

My eighth birthday, in July 1961, passed, unmarked again, in any way at all. And if I had felt special two months earlier, making my first Communion, I felt wretched and forgotten again now.

Though my own birthday was in the school summer holidays, I had seen lots of children in my class celebrating their birthdays throughout the school year. They'd skip into school showing off a new doll or a toy or a book.

"Birthday presents," they told me. "Aren't they lovely?"

One time a little girl in my class came to school in a beautiful new red coat.

"It's my birthday coat," she told me proudly, running her fingers down the sleeves.

I was so jealous; it made my heart ache.

At playtimes, we'd sing a raucous version of 'Happy Birthday' and then pull the hair of the birthday boy or girl – just like we had at home.

"Six, seven, eight!" with an extra-hard yank for the final year.

I joined in with as much enthusiasm as everyone else. But deep down, I longed for it to be me. Just once.

I did wonder too, why mum and dad had not come to see me for my birthday. Why they didn't even send me a card. I wondered whether perhaps they had sent a card, and Sister Isobel had hidden it, out of spite. I hoped this was the case. Because the alternative did not bear thinking about.

There was no let up in the abuse all through the summer but, just as before, there was no regular pattern, either. I just got used to it and got on with it. I learned to cope. My recollections of my family were becoming ever more hazy now and I relied on Winifred to keep my fading memories alive, in my mind at least. It had been over a year since I'd seen my dad, and two years since I'd seen my mum.

In the dead of night, I would lie stiff, beneath my rigid sheets, my eyes wide with fear. The fear of forgetting. And, far worse, of being forgotten.

"We're going home," I would tell Winifred. "You and me and our blue case. We're going home where we belong."

But my voice often cracked and lacked conviction. And though Winifred wore the same pleasant smile, I felt I could now see uncertainty in her round eyes.

Was she losing hope too?

* * *

Chapter Sixteen

It was late in the summer of 1961 when, as I was playing in the Reccy one Saturday, one of the big girls came over and tapped me on the shoulder.

"Message from the Mother Superior," she said. "You have a visitor, Kibby. You're wanted in the entrance hall."

I had been engrossed in a game of hide and seek. But suddenly, a thrill ran through me and I felt my heart beating faster, too fast.

"Who is it?" I asked, in a small voice.

But she just shrugged and strolled off, her job complete. With my legs like jelly, I went as quickly as I dared, along the corridors. Sister Isobel did not allow running, just as she did not allow laughing or asking questions. I didn't want to get caught and dragged away for a punishment and miss my all-important visit.

Hope surged within me, as I hurried along, that my dad might be here – here to take me home. But as I rounded the corner into the entrance hall, I was met by a whole cluster of faces, more dear to me than my own.

My mum, heavily pregnant again and with one hand on her belly, was standing next to her own mum, my Irish grandmother. And around them stood the little brothers and sisters my wounded heart had been weeping for. Peter, Christine, Johnny, Jeanie and what must be little Kathleen, toddling around, rolls of fat around her short legs, her nappy hanging somewhere by her knees. She had changed so much I did not even recognise her.

The scene, the perfect domestic bliss I had hankered after and sobbed over, was too much for me to bear.

Granny walked towards me and held out her arms and on instinct now, I held back, nervous and uncertain. I wasn't used to kindness. I wasn't used to love.

When fingers were reached out towards me, they had usually been dipped in evil first.

But my grandmother's smile was so warm and reassuring that I realised this cuddle, unlike all the others, was safe.

She took me in her arms and held me tight and I felt my whole body shake and break with sobs of happiness. Her tenderness seemed to hurt more at that point than all the beatings.

One of the nuns showed us into a small room and the door closed. Me and my family together. At last! The little ones, inquisitive and full of energy, ran around the room, picking up books, pulling at curtains, sliding across the polished floor. They ran riot. The noise was welcome, I was so thankful just to hear their voices.

"Why are you in here?" Peter asked curiously. "Have you been naughty?"

I shrugged, a little uncomfortable and embarrassed.

"Marie's been naughty!" sang the little ones. "Marie's been naughty!"

My mother, as always, was busy trying to keep the little ones in check, conscious they might damage a chair or scratch the floor. She said very little, but I could tell, as she looked around the room, that she was disapproving.

She was not happy with the convent. This was not what she had wanted for me. I felt a surge of optimism. She didn't like the place, so she was sure to want to get me out of here.

And yet, somehow, I didn't know why, I could not bring myself to ask her if she would take me home. Perhaps deep down, I already knew the answer.

She could not cope with the children she had, and she had another baby on the way. How could she possibly take me home now?

And it was easy to swallow my questions, because the little ones filled the visit with their mischief and their noise.

When it was time for them to go, the door opened and a nun nodded at my mother and I like to think that she scowled back at her.

Mum got heavily to her feet on her swollen legs, and she took my face in her hands.

"You're a good girl, Mairin," she whispered.

Hearing my name, in that way, both broke my heart and filled me with unspeakable joy. I could not bear to watch them walk away and I turned away as they filed out of the room. I heard the big doors slam shut and I had a horrible, creeping feeling, as my family left, that I was no longer part of it.

That night, in bed, I told Winifred all about the visit and, though I tried to put on a brave face, I could not help going back, in my mind, to Peter's question:

"Why are you in here?"

Had I done something wrong? Did they not love me as much? Didn't they need me any more? Perhaps Christine was now big enough to answer the door, to deal with the cruelty man and the police officers. Maybe she was old enough to 'hold the fort' for dad.

The jealousy was hot and bitter in the back of my throat.

During the visit I had been too overwhelmed to consider it, but now, cold and alone in my scratchy bed, I realised that Johnny had obviously been sent home from the convent. He was back with the family. Back in the fold.

If they had come for Johnny, why not me?

I felt a growing resentment bubbling in my throat. They all got to go home, so why not me? And what about the new baby mum was expecting? How would she manage to look after another little one, without my help? It was me who changed the nappies and pushed the pram. Not Christine. Me. Or could it rather be that the new baby was a replacement for me? A shudder ran through me.

And then, there was poor Freddie. He wasn't even included in the visit, unless they had seen him separately. Had he been left out completely?

What on earth could two little defenceless children have done that was so bad as to deserve this? We were trapped in the bowels of hell, in a temple of evil and crushing despair.

And we did not even know why.

* * *

My spirit might have decayed and died completely after mum's visit, were it not for the surprise announcement of a holiday. There was a buzz about the convent. And even some of the nuns risked a smile or a brief arm around the shoulder, when they thought Sister Isobel was not watching.

"The holiday will be in Blackpool," said Mother Superior. "At the seaside."

I had been to Ireland the previous summer, so I had no hope of being chosen again. But when my name was read out, on a short list of girls, I was stunned.

Blackpool. Blackpool!

I had never been of course, but I had heard all about it. I knew there was a funfair and a seaside. It was an actual holiday place. I thought back to Freddie and me, arriving in this hateful place – expecting a holiday – and I managed a sad smile.

Already, at the age of eight, I was world-weary and wise to it all.

Just being on a bus, away from the convent, was exhilarating. I felt a pang of guilt, leaving Freddie behind. But I had no control over what happened to him, and no way of knowing too if he had even been on holiday already – without me. And I was learning slowly, very slowly, to quietly accept the things I could not change and keep myself out of trouble.

I was learning to disappear. Not to be me.

We arrived in Blackpool, with the taste of salty air on our tongues and the stiff breeze from the sea sending our hair wild. We were staying in a small guesthouse, overlooking the sea front. It was a treat for me just to have a window to look out of.

The bigger girls were on the trip – of course they were – and they took every opportunity to push me about, tease me, trip me up and get me into trouble.

"Let's throw Kibby in the sea," laughed one. "Pick her up and chuck her in the water. See if she can swim all the way back to her family."

"Course she can't," replied another. "She *has* no family. Remember?"

My cheeks burned but I bit back my tears and said nothing. I stared outside, at the waves crashing in the distance, and pictured myself holding their heads under water, one by one, until I had drowned them all.

I did at least think that the Blackpool trip might give me a few days break from the abuse. One of the younger nuns was sleeping in our bedroom and I felt quietly confident that they wouldn't try anything too revolting, with her nearby. Though she had never been kind to me, she had never been mean to me, either. So whilst she wasn't on my side, she certainly wasn't on theirs. There were other holidaymakers in the guesthouse too, as well as the staff. Somehow, I didn't think Sister Isobel would want her dirty secrets hung out to dry in the Blackpool breeze.

So for the first time in years, I felt quite safe.

The guesthouse was run by a family and their teenage daughter, Elizabeth, for some reason, took me under her wing.

"Those girls are horrible to you," she said. "They're bullies. I don't know how they're allowed to get away with it."

It was something I had never really thought about. Far from getting away with it, they were actively encouraged, by Sister Isobel. But I didn't tell her that.

"It's not right," Elizabeth said again.

When we went out later, for a walk along the beach, Elizabeth stood at the door and waved and I found myself waving and smiling back at her.

A small part of me was a little bit scared. Why was she being so friendly? I just wasn't used to it and it made me suspicious. In my experience, people only ever pretended to be nice, so that the bombshell they later dropped was twice as shocking.

That night, Elizabeth called me to her room, and I was wary.

"What for?" I asked anxiously.

"Look," she replied, pointing to a row of nail varnish bottles. "I can't decide which colour to wear and I wanted your opinion. If you don't mind."

My opinion! I was bowled over. I couldn't remember the last time anyone had been interested in what I had to say. I pointed to a pretty pink bottle and I tried to smile, but to my dismay, a tear rolled down my cheek and splashed onto the carpet.

I didn't know why I was crying. I was happier than I'd been for months. I had a real friend.

The next day, at breakfast, we were served bacon and eggs and offered a choice of cereals. A choice! I had automatically picked up my empty plate, ready to form a queue for breakfast. But Elizabeth saw me and laughed.

"Sit down," she said. "I'll bring the food to your table. You're in a hotel. That's how it works."

I couldn't believe my luck. I felt like I was playing a part in a film. I felt like I was posh!

Later, we were taken back to the beach for a shoot with a press photographer. We were instructed all to smile and run at the camera, in a long line, linking arms, as though we were having the time of our lives.

"Smile!" Sister Isobel ordered, with a face like thunder.

It was as though we were being condemned.

"She just wants everyone to think we're having a great time at the convent," hissed one of the older girls. "It's all a show. All a big act."

But I didn't care. I had a friend. Someone who wanted my opinion. Someone who wanted to hear my thoughts.

That afternoon, we were taken up to the top of Blackpool Tower. I looked out, across the rooftops and the chimneys, and I wondered if one of those houses was mine.

Somehow, 518 metres up there in the sky, I felt much closer to Oldham.

"Can they see me?" I wondered. "Can they see Blackpool Tower?"

I half-expected a reply from our street. But there was nothing except the screeching of the seagulls and the faint noise of the traffic below.

On our last night in Blackpool, I lay in bed, listening to the dregs of the drinkers staggering home through the streets outside, and I wrestled with my mind.

I desperately wanted to tell Elizabeth about the convent. About the abuse. Sister Isobel. The big girls. The coat-hangers. The 'kissing French boys'.

She had already noticed how horrid they were. It was as if she was paving the way for me to spill my secret.

It was a cumbersome, crushing, weight for me to carry around all on my own. It cast a darkness, a deep sadness, over everything I did. And I wanted so much to share it.

Elizabeth, like the little boy from the playground, was a true friend. That night the two of them weaved in and out of my dreams, holding my head above the waves as I bobbed up and down in the Irish sea, wearing my starchy nightdress and a large pair of black boots.

At first the sea was calm and Elizabeth and the little boy laughed and splashed as we swam further out to sea. But I could feel my boots filling with seawater, growing heavy and dragging me down.

"Help!" I called, as my head disappeared under the water. "Help! I'm drowning. And you're my only friends."

Elizabeth and the little boy did their best to grab me but the waves buffeted them back and I slipped from their grasp. I felt myself sinking, and I tried desperately to kick off the black boots which I knew were pulling me under.

But once under the water, I could see my white legs, kicking furiously, under the nightdress. And I realised, in horror, that they were not boots at all. They were two black sleeves, and two veiny hands, gripping my feet and dragging me further and further towards the seabed. I knew who the arms belonged to, even before I saw the pinched, razor-sharp features.

"Please, Sister Isobel, I'm drowning," I pleaded.

But as I opened my mouth, there was no sound. Only bubbles. And then a blackness wrapped itself around me.

The next morning, the seagulls woke me early. Even the relief of realising I was still in Blackpool, away from the chores and the prayers of the convent, was not enough to cheer me up. And despite a wonderful cooked breakfast, I could not shake the uneasiness.

Chapter Sixteen

I wanted so much to tell Elizabeth. I really did.

But afterwards, as we chatted in her bedroom, I found that the words just stuck in my throat. In fact, I didn't even have any words. I didn't know how or where to start.

"It's been so lovely to meet you," she beamed, and she threw her arms around me. "I won't ever forget you, my little friend."

We said goodbye. And I carried my burden back to the convent – alone.

Chapter Seventeen

A little like the visits from home, the trip to Blackpool – while lovely – only served to emphasise the agony of my daily existence. I had nothing – nothing whatsoever – to look forward to.

November 5 1961 came, and this time we were taken out in a long, regimented line, two by two, to a local bonfire. It was an exciting night for me, even under the critical eye of Sister Isobel. We were herded into the park where a huge bonfire was already burning. A volunteer handed sparklers around, and I lit my sparkler off the tip of Dil's.

We laughed and shouted as we wrote in the air from the beam of our sparklers. Dil tried to write: 'Happy Bonfire Night' but her sparkler burned out at 'Bonf' and 'Bonfir' each time.

With a little of my old defiance returning, I scrawled: 'Marie' across the night sky, stretching my arm high and wide with the sparklers, in letters as big and proud as I could make them.

Yes, that was my name. That was who I was. Maybe they would even see the golden letters back home in Oldham. I had a rush of happiness as I gazed at the fire.

Then as I turned to smile at Dil, I saw that her pale face was lit up by the flames, and in the darkness, she looked ghoulish and translucent.

And my whole body prickled with abhorrence.

This was the girl who had climbed into my bed, clamped her mouth on mine and sexually assaulted me in the darkness. Now here I was, sharing sparklers and jokes with her.

What had become of me? What had they made me into?

I sank onto my knees in the mud, drained of energy, as the misery enveloped me once again.

That Christmas, we trooped off into town again for our annual festive shopping expedition. I loved those trips. But, now that I was getting older, I was starting to question how, on the one hand, the nuns had told me I had no family. But yet at Christmas, I was allowed to buy a present for a family member.

It was either one. Or the other. Nuns, I knew, were not supposed to be untruthful. Nuns were not supposed to commit sins. And yet there was much that went on in the convent that didn't seem strictly in keeping with their religious vows.

I saw the trip into town as a chink in the façade, a crack in the lies. It was, surely, an admission that I did have a family. And I did have a home.

The day of our outing in December 1961 dawned and the children were at fever pitch.

"I'm getting chocolates for my granny," said one girl.

"I've no family," said another little girl, even smaller than I was. "Nobody to buy anything for."

It was a tragic moment, but in the convent we lived on tragedy, day in, day out. There were kids who feasted on it. Certainly, there were no strangers to heartache and hardship here. And so there was little sympathy for the poor little girl who had nobody to buy for in the whole world.

"Well if you've got no-one, you can keep your chocolates all for yourself then can't you, fatty!" retorted one of the big girls and we all laughed as we lined up, ready to leave. I laughed along with them. I had to. Or it would be me in the firing line next.

"Quiet, girls," shrieked Sister Isobel, a warning cane in her hand.

We linked arms, two by two, a big girl with a little one. The nuns brought up the rear of the procession. But even from the very back of the line, I could feel their breath, red-hot like dragon fire.

"Behave girls," hissed Sister Isobel. "Or else."

It never ceased to amaze me how the nuns transformed from overbearing bullies inside the convent walls, into smiling, charming, women as soon as we were on the outside. They almost became maternal.

It was always more awkward, admittedly, for Sister Isobel. Hers was more of a mutation into something slightly less scary but, in my mind, undeniably deviant.

But for the other nuns, it was a true metamorphosis.

"Come on, children," they beamed, one holding a grateful hand out to stop the traffic while the others ushered us across the main street in St Helens. Like mother ducks with a precious brood.

"Off we go, now!"

This year, I had decided to buy something for my dad. And after careful deliberation in the posh department store, the very same shop where I had picked out mum's perfume, I chose a small box with two handkerchiefs inside. One white, one pale blue.

"He will love these," I said dreamily.

I liked the little box even more than the hankies themselves. And I could just see my dad, prancing around the living room with one in his top pocket. Acting the fool and telling a funny story, just like he always did. I had never even seen him wear a tie, he was always in his workman's gear, so I knew these would be a real treat for him.

The gifts were packaged and posted and I hoped – yearned – for a reply. I'd have settled for a snotty hanky, back in the post. But I got nothing.

Christmas week brought another visit from Santa and by now I was well used to the drill. There was a clamour amongst the little ones as soon as they spotted the sack of gifts, but I hung back, unimpressed. I wanted to be cool, to fit in with the older kids, and it wasn't the done thing at eight years of age to throw myself at a fake Santa.

I received my present along with the others and tried to feign disinterest when I unwrapped a woollen scarf. But deep down, my heart leapt as I slipped it round my neck. It almost felt like a cuddle.

And it wasn't so much the scarf. It was the fact that someone had wrapped it for me. Someone had taken time, trouble and care. For me.

It was the thoughtfulness, the love behind the gift, that really touched me. Kindness was a bigger killer than cruelty and, as I wrapped the scarf around my cherished Winifred in bed that night, I dissolved into lonely tears.

As I lay in the half-light, I remembered an afternoon from my last Christmas at home, when me and Johnny had made paper chains, each looped into the next, to hang across the ceiling, as decorations.

We found a packet of cotton wool, probably bought for nappy changing, and hung clumps on the Christmas tree, to look like snow.

I even drew a fairy on the inside of an old cereal packet and we cut her out and stuck her on the top.

I pictured Johnny, clapping his hands together, his face lit up with appreciation.

"It's fantastic," he kept saying. "Love it! Love it Marie!"

With his blonde curls and his cherubic cheeks, he looked a little bit like baby Jesus and we used to joke that he could be the real live baby in a Christmas crib. To me, he had an exquisite, gorgeous, innocence. It was almost other-worldly.

A little while later, Johnny was playing with the embers in the coal fire, shovelling little scraps from the hearth, back into the fire.

Somehow, whilst nobody was really paying attention, one of the embers must have floated onto the Christmas tree and it quickly caught fire. Within a few minutes it was ablaze and dad rushed in, grabbed it by the base, and ran into the back yard, hollering.

The tree was dumped in the coal shed and doused with water. And all that was left, afterwards, was a burnt stalk and a terrible smell.

Poor Johnny was inconsolable, his chubby face crumpled with guilt and smeared with tears and black coal marks.

"What about the fairy?" he asked. "Did she die in the fire?"

"No," dad told him with a smile. "The fairy flew off to heaven. She's absolutely fine."

In the end, to cheer him up, I sat him on my knee and we all sang *Away in a Manger*. That night, in bed, there were coal stains all over the pillow.

What I missed at Christmas, more than anything, was the togetherness.

✳ ✳ ✳

One Saturday morning, early in the New Year of 1962, the snow came. There was no window in my bedroom and so it wasn't until we filed into the dining room for breakfast that we got a good view of the thick carpet of snow, covering the grounds outside. It was still falling too – good-sized flakes, ideal for snowballs.

"Perfect," I said with a smile.

Like excited ants we scurried over to the windows and gazed outside.

"Sit!" Sister Isobel commanded.

As though we were on remote control, we all turned and walked back to our tables in silence. But when breakfast was over, the racket began again.

"Can we play out? Please Sister? Please?"

Sister Isobel raised her hand for silence and again, the effect was instant. Her thin lips settled briefly into a monstrous smile, as though she was enjoying every minute.

"There will be no outdoor play," she said. "Nobody will leave the building."

A collective groan rippled through the crowd but nobody was stupid enough to challenge her. Yet it seemed so unfair.

"You will instead be allowed to play in the recreation room," she added.

That was exactly how she liked it. Orderly, restrained, pious children having orderly restrained, pious fun.

In the Reccy that afternoon, there was hardly a free spot by the windows. We all looked out, longingly, at the white blanket outside. It was a day of missed opportunities. Of what might have been.

I thought back to the snow at home and my heart ached. In Oldham we always got lots of snow in the winter; sometimes as much as three feet, stacked up against the back door.

As the first flakes started to fall, we'd race out into the street, throwing snowballs and carrying a home-made sledge. It was a free for all. Kids screaming, laughing and bursting with fun. Our fingers were red raw with the cold, our shoes were soaked through, but none of that mattered.

When there was a good covering, enough to sledge, we all trudged up a nearby hill and took it in turns to skid down and make what we called a 'Slippy Curry' – literally a slide made from ice. By the time it was ready for the sledges, it was lethal.

It really felt as if we were flying. I would sit on the back of the sledge, with three little ones on the front, holding on for dear life. There were bust lips and black eyes and even the odd broken leg. But there was so much joy, too.

Then, there were snowman competitions, to see who could build the biggest and best on the street. And of course our family, with so many kids, always won hands down.

"Coal for eyes, carrot for a nose, old bobble hat to keep his head warm," I would say, and the little ones would scarper off in different directions to find what we needed.

The finished product was always, always, splendid.

Sitting in the Reccy, at the convent, I was warm and dry.

But I would have swapped it all in an instant. I'd have given anything for a twisted ankle and one last turn down a Slippy Curry.

* * *

It was well into January, as I ate breakfast one morning, that I felt a shooting pain at the back of my mouth. I almost cried out in pain but I knew better, by now. As the day went on, it became a dull ache, and I felt sickly and unwell. All night, my mouth pounded and throbbed. Tears dribbled down my face and onto the stiff, unforgiving sheets. Tears for my pain. And tears for my loneliness.

The fact that nobody knew, or cared, that I was ill was much worse than the pain itself. I felt crushed.

The next morning, when the bell went, I did not feel well enough even to lift my head from the pillow. I was almost delirious with exhaustion and pain. But I knew, in total certainty, that if I didn't get up, I would be in for a hiding.

Over the months, I had seen girls literally heaving themselves out of bed, crawling through their chores and their prayers. Because the fear of Sister Isobel and her burning wrath was worse than any injury or any illness.

Chapter Seventeen

"Your face is fatter at one side than the other," Dil remarked, as if it was a party trick.

My mouth was so sore I could not bear to wash my face. And at breakfast, when I sat down with my porridge, I could not manage even a mouthful.

"What's the matter child?" demanded Sister Isobel.

I lifted my head and she nodded, as if that in itself was sufficient explanation. She placed a hand on my forehead and nodded again in self-congratulation.

"You're running a fever and your face is swollen," she told me. "Have you got toothache?"

I thought for a moment and realised this was exactly the problem.

"Yes," I replied.

But then a split second later, a horrible thought hit me and I added: "Please, Sister, can I go to school. I am not ill."

The prospect of being left in the convent as easy prey was worse than any toothache. I would have dragged myself to school on my hands and knees if necessary.

Somehow, I made it through the day at school but by the end, I was hot and nauseous and my whole face pulsed with pain. Even so, the next morning, I was made to scrub the floors and wash and pray, as usual. I was barely lucid as I made my way into the dining room for breakfast.

I was slumped forward, staring at my porridge, when Dil whispered:

"Head up, here comes Sister Isobel."

I was aware of her standing behind me, as she tapped me on the shoulder and informed me I would be missing school that day.

"Wait here, child," she told me. "And be quiet."

I didn't want to miss school. I knew this had to be some sort of trap. Back at home, when I was ill, mum would tuck me into the big bed, bring a cup of warm milk and sing her famous lullabies. The little ones would buzz in and out of the bedroom, bringing snippets of information from the day.

"Peter banged his head. Kathleen has been sick all over the couch. Christine says she's the prettiest of us all."

Despite my sore throat or my bruised knee, I felt happy and safe in that bed. I felt loved and wanted.

But I knew it would not be like that here. In the convent, being ill was worthy of punishment. Just like everything else. The dining room emptied out, and my mood sank. What did Sister Isobel have in store for me today?

But then, one of the younger nuns came into the room and I saw, in excitement, that she was wearing a coat. We were going out!

"Get your outdoor things," she said, clipping every word. "Meet me in the entrance hall."

I couldn't wait. Wherever we were going, it was an escape. And that was good enough for me. We walked out of the convent, onto the road, and waited by the bus stop. Suddenly feeling brighter in the fresh air, I was hopping from one foot to the other, looking forward to my day.

"Keep still," snapped the nun. "And stay close to me."

She didn't let me move more than a couple of feet away from her and I wondered whether she thought I might run away. The idea ran briefly through my mind. But it was no more than that – an idea. I didn't even know which way was home. Besides, I wasn't sure I could actually run at all, the way I was feeling.

The bus came, and I clambered on, and the nun squashed me into the window seat so that I could barely move an inch, never mind wriggle away from her. As we rumbled on, through the streets, past the dingy looking houses, a memory flashed into my mind.

It had been a cold, miserable day, driving with rain, but we needed to go to the market for food. Mum took all seven of us with her, and we made a dripping and rather dreary spectacle, running along the aisles and jumping onto the seats at the back. Freddie and me hoisted Peter up the steps, with his bad leg, and then lifted the little ones up next to us.

It was a treat, going on a bus, and Peter was singing loudly. The rest of us were peering out of the back window, waving at the cars, pulling funny faces at passers-by.

When the conductor came round, mum nodded awkwardly at baby Kathleen, on her knee, and mumbled: "One and a half."

"What about these?" he asked, nodding towards Freddie, Peter, Christine, Jeanie, Johnny and me.

She scrambled in her purse for a few moments and the anxiety hung there, in the air. Peter abruptly stopped singing. My heart felt suddenly heavy.

"I can't afford to pay," she said in a whisper. "I'm sorry."

The conductor had the air of a man who had seen it all before and was not too interested either way. He just nodded and moved onto the next passenger. But my poor mother was mortified. She wasn't someone who accepted charity easily and yet much of the time she had no choice.

There were a couple of passengers in front who turned to us with pitying smiles. A woman further up tutted loudly at my mother.

"It's OK, mum," I said, taking her hand in mine. "We got on the bus for free!"

"We've still got to get home again," she replied dully, with her blank eyes.

Days like that had seemed truly awful to me, back then. I had thought, as my mother did, that life had dealt us a rotten hand. But now, as I stared out of the bus window, with the nun squeezing me against the glass, and my mouth starting to throb again, I realised I had been lacking perspective somewhat.

At home, I had felt I had grown up quickly, too quickly. I took responsibility, I helped with childcare, I dealt with the cruelty man. But now, at the convent, my childhood and my innocence had been brutally stamped out and snatched away for good.

Perhaps, I reasoned, it was only possible to truly appreciate what we had, when it was taken away. I hoped that somewhere, my mother was learning the same, harsh lesson.

* * *

Our stop came and the nun stood up and gave my shoulder a shake. She hadn't spoken to me during the entire journey.

"So where are we going?" I asked, as we walked along the street.

"Dentist," she replied.

Although I knew they looked after teeth, I couldn't remember ever seeing a dentist before. So that didn't really help much at all.

We arrived at the surgery and I was taken in to see the dentist himself. I hopped up into the chair and it was so big, it almost swallowed me. I caught sight of his metal instruments, glinting in a tray beside me, and I felt a terrified thrill.

They were surely too big for my tiny mouth! Was this going to hurt? He poked around inside my mouth for a few minutes before having a quiet conversation with the waiting nun. When he came back, he clamped a gas mask over my mouth and I panicked, instantly, that he was trying to kill me, that this was just another aspect of Sister Isobel's evil regime.

I fought as hard as I could, maybe for a few seconds, before I began to feel woozy and sick.

As the gas oozed into my bloodstream, I could see giant, ten feet crows, wearing veils and long habits, strutting about our living room in Oldham and screeching: "Christine, hold the baby! Christine, burp the baby! Christine, you're our right-hand man now!"

I wriggled, trying to get up, but it felt as though I was being pinned down on the chair. And then, total panic, as the gloating and greedy faces of the big girls loomed over mine, their teeth dripping blood, their eyes like slits in curtains.

"Aw, in't she lovely," they cooed, in voices that sounded just like baby Kathleen. "In't she smashing? Let's cut her hair and teach her how to kiss French boys."

When I came around, groggy and disorientated, and frightened half to death, I was weeping. My mouth was packed with tissue and my jaw throbbed.

"We've taken a bad tooth out," the dentist explained kindly. "You've been a brave girl."

But the nun sat, impassive, on the chair and said nothing. The visit left me with a life-long terror of dentists. To add to my life-long terror of nuns.

Chapter Eighteen

Once a week, perhaps it was a Saturday, some of the children in the convent received letters in the post. Occasionally, some got parcels from family or friends. I would drool with envy as I watched them scurry off with their letter or their present, to read and enjoy in peace.

Where were mine? Why didn't my family ever write?

It wasn't so much that I wanted a gift. I knew my parents couldn't afford that, especially not, I remembered with a crackle of annoyance, that they had a new baby to look after. A new baby to take my place. But I would have liked a letter or a postcard. I wanted to hear news from home, of course I did. But more than that, I needed to know that I was not forgotten. Not replaced.

But one such Saturday, as Sister Isobel sorted through the pile of letters, she said:

"Kibby, here's one for you."

Her voice was dripping with barely disguised disgust, as if I was not worth a letter all to myself. She chucked it at me like it was litter. I gritted my teeth to thank her politely and then vanished into my room, a place I hated, a place riddled with nightmarish memories of torture and pain, but the only place I could have a moment of peace.

Opening the letter, I scanned it quickly to the bottom, and read: "All my love, Mairin, Your Mum." I gasped, overwhelmed. A letter from home!

"Your dad is busy painting the house," she wrote.

Instantly, my spirits soared. He was getting the house ready – ready for me to come home! She didn't say so, exactly. But that must surely be her meaning. He was painting the house, and they were planning my homecoming – the prodigal daughter, back at last.

Her letter continued.

"And I have been busy looking after your brothers and sisters, including our new baby Teresa." And as quickly as I was up, I was down again. The new baby was a little girl – the perfect exchange for me. Like for like. Mum was busy, busy with everyone else. Too busy for me.

I read and re-read the short letter, hoping for something I had missed. I could not decide whether the news was good or not. In any case, I slid it back inside the envelope and stashed it carefully in the blue vanity case.

When the house was painted, and they came for me, I was ready. Always, I was ready.

* * *

In the days and weeks afterwards, I hoped, desperately, that something else might happen. Another letter or a phone call. A visit from home. Or, in my wildest, most extravagant fantasies, my dad would arrive, with his kind face, and say:

"Come on then, Mairin. It's time to take you and our Freddie back home."

One or two children did go home. New ones arrived. But nothing happened for me. I settled back into the drudgery and despair of convent life.

My ninth birthday arrived, in July 1962, and there was still not even a card from my family. The agony was indescribable. My letter had been nothing more than a sip of water in a hot desert. I felt I was losing all hope now.

In many ways, I was angry and frustrated with myself. I had learned, over a period of almost three years in the convent, to pack away all my hopes and expectations, and keep them in the blue case, alongside the plastic bracelet and the pencils. I knew it did me no good to flirt with notions of home and happiness. Instead, I had perfected the art of keeping my questions to myself, asking for little, and expecting even less.

I had learned how to play the game.

But the letter had reawakened all the old feelings, and I had dared to dream once more. It was a dangerous trap and I was determined never to fall into it again.

* * *

The Convent

One morning in August, I woke to the sound of Sister Isobel's bell, and I heard noises down the corridor of frightened children frantically making their beds and scurrying out into the corridor to pray.

I knew I had to get up. I heard the door creak and Dil poked her head in.

"Come on," she whispered. "Hurry up, Kibby."

But I could not. I was not tired or sick or rebellious. Strangely, I felt like I was pinned to the bed, held in place as surely as though I had bricks piled on my chest. My breath came in short, shallow, uneven bursts and I was gripped by an overwhelming, paralysing feeling of dread.

I knew that I was a sitting duck. I knew I was for it. And sure enough, moments later, I heard Sister Isobel's bloodthirsty shoes clacking their way, along the floors, towards me.

"Where's Kibby?" she rasped.

I heard the girls in the corridor whimpering in reply, before she marched into the room and loomed over me like a great tower of righteous evil.

"Get out of bed," she said quietly.

Her voice was barely audible and terrified me more than if she had screamed at the top of her lungs.

I could not move. And I also could not speak. I just stared, mute, wide-eyed. My heart was thumping so hard I knew, even at that age, that it was not healthy.

There were ten seconds, maybe, of silence. But it felt like a year. Waiting, waiting, waiting.

And then, she snapped.

"Get up!" she screeched. "Get up!"

She pulled back the sheets and pulled me, by my hair, onto the floor. I was aware that I was scrambling automatically into a ball, for self-preservation, as I always did. But somehow, I didn't feel like it was me doing the movements. It was as though someone was pulling my strings and I was just a puppet.

Sister Isobel barked a command and a crowd of bigger girls rushed in, savagely thrilled by the unexpected prospect of early-morning entertainment.

I felt the kicks and punches. I heard them laugh and saw the spit flying from their mouths. But this time none of it felt real. None of it felt like it was happening – really happening – to me.

"Leave her," came the next order and the girls fled, just as terrified in their own way of Sister Isobel, as I was.

I was left on the floor, with my eyes swelling and my legs stinging, whilst the other children said their prayers, scrubbed the floors, and went for breakfast.

I could not have eaten anyway. I was past that. In many ways, I felt like I could take no more. Deep inside, I wondered whether I would first have to be completely broken into pieces, in order for me to be rebuilt from scratch once again.

Perhaps this was all part of the process. Or perhaps the recovery had started, and I just didn't know it.

Or maybe, yes more likely, this numbness was the beginning of the end of me.

* * *

The following morning, I was allowed back at breakfast, with the strange episode still weighing massively on my mind. But there was a buzz amongst the children, which always suggested there was new gossip to be had. And despite my debilitating bout of whatever it was, I was edging closer to join in, despite myself.

"You won't believe this," said one of the girls. "The convent is closing down! It's actually closing! All the kids who can't move to Liverpool have got to go home!"

I felt like all my insides had been liquidised. Like someone had opened a trapdoor and all my internal organs had just shot out.

"Am I going home?" I asked, weakly. "Can I go too?"

"You have no home, Kibby," snorted one of the big girls, and they all started to laugh, as if it was their long-running prank. Like I really should have been able to see the funny side myself by now.

My mind was whirring at a million miles an hour. Surely if the convent was closing, I would have to go home? Mum and dad couldn't – wouldn't – send me to Liverpool. I had no idea where it was, I had never even heard of it, but I was pretty sure it was nowhere near Oldham.

I spotted Sister Isobel, at the far corner of the room, rapping a quivering and unfortunate hand with her cane. I knew this was not a good time to try to talk to her.

Chapter Eighteen

"Home!" I said to myself. "Am I going back to my family?"

Those two words, alien and painful to me for so long, now suddenly tripped lovingly off the end of my tongue.

I was forced to wait.

But I was hardly able to contain myself. I felt like a mini volcano, about to erupt and explode with the pressure. It went round and round my head. It had been three years since I had seen my home. Three long years since I had slept in my own bed, skipped down my street, played with my brothers and sisters and my pals.

It had been over a year since I had seen my mum and siblings, and even longer since I'd had the visit from my dad. And of course, I had a baby sister who I had never even met. I was awash with nerves, excitement, trepidation and joy.

"What if they won't have you back, Marie?" asked a peevish voice in my head. "What if they don't want you?

"Christine is the right-hand man now. They have a new daughter, too, to take your place. What if you're no longer needed?"

I pushed the voice out, clapping my hands over my ears. The wait was unbearable. I had to know.

The rumours and the gossip continued all day.

"It's closing. We're leaving tonight."

"No it isn't. It's never closing. We're here for the rest of our lives."

That night we went to the Reccy and some of the boys got into a fight. It wasn't unusual for the boys to scrap and wrestle in the Reccy and sometimes it was a welcome diversion. We'd all stand around and chant and cheer until one of the nuns arrived to give them all a smart smack on the backside with a cane.

Punishment for us all was a decade of the Rosary, said while facing the wall, and "showing remorse". I never really understood what that meant, but I always made sure my eyes were tightly closed as I mumbled my way through my prayers, so that I could not be accused of failing to show the required measure of contrition.

But tonight, I could not bring myself to concentrate on the brawl. I could think only of home. Of Christine, telling me how pretty she was. Of plump little Johnny twisting his fingers around his curls. Of dad in his overalls, pushing his cart. Of mum in her coat with the round chocolatey buttons.

I thought too, of the little boy in the playground and of Elizabeth at the guesthouse. My two true friends. Thoughts of them had seen me through some dark days in this convent. And I would rely on them both now to get me through whatever was coming next.

Chapter Nineteen

The next morning at breakfast, Sister Isobel blew a whistle and the place fell silent just as though we had all been turned to stone.

"I have an announcement to make," she began, and a ripple of anxiety ran through me. I was hardly able to bring myself to listen.

"Our order of nuns will be moving to Liverpool soon," she announced. "The convent will be closing. Those of you who cannot move to Liverpool will be going home if, indeed," – and here her lip curled – "you have a home to go to."

I felt as though my heart had stopped beating. The apprehension, the expectation in the room was palpable.

"What about me? Where am I going?"

There were dozens of children. All wanting the right answer. The only answer. I felt sick inside. This was it.

Sister Isobel was taken up dealing with other children at first, and it gave me a chance to get my breath back. However, she gave each one a short, sharp reply and it was soon my turn to speak.

"Will I be going home please, Sister?" I asked.

I felt as though I had spoken in slow-motion, as if the world was shuddering to a halt on its axis. As though the next moment would go down in global history.

"Yes, you will, Kibby," she replied, looking as though the thought pained her. As though I really was getting a treat I didn't deserve.

The words washed over me like soothing balm. Like the answer I had been looking for all of my life. I could see – actually see – the hope, shimmering in the air above me like fine strands of gold.

"When?" I asked. "When can I go?"

I was babbling now, excited. The world was turning again, speeding now, helter-skelter, fast and frantic. I almost felt like I might fall off if I didn't hang on tight.

"When? When? When?"

Sister Isobel turned and snarled, and I knew I had gone too far.

"You would do well to remember that you are a child of God," she barked.

She grabbed hold of the back of my jumper and lifted me bodily off the ground.

"You will go home when you have learned to stop asking questions," she breathed into my ear.

The punishment did nothing to dampen my joy. Nothing could have upset me.

Chapter Nineteen

"We're going home, Dil," I whispered, as we filed out of the dining room.

But she shook her head.

"Not me," she said softly. "I'm going to Liverpool."

"But why?" I began, and then I saw the shame and the pain on her face, and I swallowed my question.

"Only those of you who have homes to go to," Sister Isobel had said.

And Dil obviously didn't. I'd spent the last three years insisting that I wasn't an orphan. It had become a dirty word, a crippling affliction, in my mind.

And yet, Dil was an orphan herself. A real one. She had nobody. I felt a rush of gratitude and goodwill, as though I was the luckiest girl in the world, because I had a family. I wanted to put my arms around Dil and give her a cuddle, but I had learned, from bitter experience, that wasn't a good idea in this place. My hands hung loosely by my sides and the right words to comfort her, whatever they were, never came.

When bedtime came that night, I pulled my little blue case from under my mattress and checked everything. It was all there. Ready and waiting.

The mood around the convent for the next few days was a strange one. Some kids were on cloud nine; making plans, packing bags, ready for home. They were giggly and excited, and it spilled over at mealtimes.

"Won't be eating this crap for much longer," whispered one girl as we queued for porridge.

"I can't wait to see my Mam and my little dog. Can't wait!"

For others, the announcement had been nothing more than a twist of the knife, a reminder of what could have been. For them, a move to a new convent meant nothing. The scenery was changing but the characters were staying the same. And Sister Isobel, the villain of the piece, would have the same starring and sickening role.

I tried to temper my enthusiasm, but I was a nine-year-old girl, brimming with joy, and I just couldn't help it. I found the big girls chatting in the Reccy and announced:

"I'm going home! I do have a home and I do have a family, after all."

I had a hand on my hip and I did the nearest thing I dared to a smirk.

"There's time for one more beating, Kibby, before yer leave," snapped one of the girls, making a lunge towards me.

I fled, but with a smile on my face. The fear was no longer there. I felt as though I finally had the upper hand. As though the tide was finally turning. For me.

* * *

It was possibly two weeks from Sister Isobel's announcement until the Big Day itself. Each night, I would lie in bed, whispering to Winifred, and filling her in on life at home.

"It's a squash in the bed," I warned her. "But it's comfy and warm and it's a good giggle as well. There's another dolly there called Winifred, just like you.

"I'm sorry I called you both Winifred, I suppose I didn't think you would ever meet one another. But it's too late now. And I think you'll both be friends.

"There's not much money but that doesn't matter. And wait till you hear Peter's jokes, and you listen to dad's stories from the war. And you'll see our Jeanie, and Johnny, and Kathleen.

"You'll love it, Winifred, you really will."

I felt a niggle of apprehension as I remembered that there was a new baby girl in the family – someone I had never even met. Someone who might be my replacement.

"I hope they still want me back," I murmured, more to myself than to Winifred. "I hope I'm not forgotten."

In the daytimes, I was as inconspicuous and demure as I could possibly be. I had all but zipped up my mouth and closed off my mind. I was determined not to do anything – anything at all – to jeopardise my chances of going home.

In darker moments, I would have flashes of anxiety that Sister Isobel might change her mind and cart me off to Liverpool, kicking and screaming, with my poor family watching on, helpless, from afar.

But she seemed, for the most part, to reserve her vitriol for the children who were staying with the convent. It was as if her job was done and her interest in me had waned. I had outlived my purpose.

It struck me also that, in those final days, there were no beatings and there was no more sexual abuse. At the time, I thought I was on barley, like it was a big game of hide and seek and I had special permission not to play.

And when I recall it now, I still believe I had special status – but not for the reasons I had thought back then. They left me alone, I think, because I was no longer afraid and vulnerable. I was no longer easy prey, easy pickings. I had a confidence, a jauntiness and it was new and probably disturbing for the people who had bullied and belittled me for so long.

The fear factor had gone. And I was finding myself once again.

The big day, when it came, in October 1962, was not the mass exodus, the biblical upheaval, that I had expected. Somehow, because it was such an earth-shattering moment in my life, I had expected the physical equivalent at the convent. I was almost surprised when the ground did not open to swallow Sister Isobel whole on my last day. I was braced for an earthquake, or a hurricane, or a parting of the seas. Something momentous to mark the hideous, horrible, trauma I had suffered for so long.

Instead, it began like any other, with glutinous porridge. Children had been leaving all that week, in dribs and drabs and without much fuss, celebration or commiseration. They were not missed and nor would they miss us. But after breakfast, Sister Isobel glowered in my direction.

Chapter Nineteen

"Get your belongings together, Kibby," she said. "You will be leaving today."

I did not speak but I beamed, from ear to ear. My heart was singing, cheering, applauding – loud within my chest. As I left the table, I caught sight of Dil, staring forlornly ahead, but it was only enough to dent my euphoria for a second.

"Bye Dil," I said, almost under my breath.

And that was that. It was like a throwaway comment. I had learned, in this place, to look after myself and nobody else. And the truth was, I didn't care about anyone I was leaving behind. I wouldn't miss any of them one bit. Freddie, I presumed, would be meeting me in the entrance hall, ready for our journey home. And the rest of them, as far I was concerned, could rot in hell.

My hands shook as I pulled out my vanity case. I packed Winifred and then my nightdress, my change of underwear and my washbag. I didn't want any reminders from the convent – least of all the scratchy nightie – but I hoped it might impress my parents that I was arriving home almost self-sufficient, as I saw it.

Sister Isobel bustled into the bedroom impatiently, and said:

"Come on now, Kibby, the car is waiting, don't show such impertinence, child. You're an ungrateful wretch. Will you never learn?"

I had done nothing wrong and I was baffled, but I made sure my facial muscles did not move an inch. I could not blow it – not now. I left the room, which had been like a crucifixion chamber for me, without so much as a backward glance. We had read, in religious studies at school, a story about a poor lady who had looked over her shoulder and been turned into a pillar of salt.

I didn't want to risk it.

Sister Isobel clack-clacked along the dark corridors, past the statues, past the stained-glass windows, past the tightly closed doors of the tiny torture rooms where my innocence had been so brutally ripped to shreds.

Arms and legs flailing. Screams of terror. And the wooden coat hangers…

I closed my mind to the images and kept my focus. I was determined not to think of it today.

In the entrance hall were two women, different to the ones who had brought me to the convent but I knew, from the pleated skirts and the sanctimonious smiles, that these were social workers. I could smell it on them.

"Off you go, Kibby," said Sister Isobel. "And be a good girl, now. Always remember – always – you are a child of God."

Her tone was benign, to impress the social workers, but there was menace in her voice. It was almost as if she was goading me, daring me to step out of line. But I'd had over three years of brutal boot-camp training and I nodded politely before following the women outside.

Once the fresh air hit me, and the big doors slammed behind me, I felt almost drunk with triumph. I wanted to scream and sing and yell with a euphoric jubilance, so potent that it was almost scaring me. My legs felt as though they wanted to dance, all of their own accord and my arms were straining to punch the air in victory, but I took deep breaths and walked stiffly and sedately to the waiting car.

One of the women opened the back door and said: "We're taking you home today, Marie.

"It's a long journey mind, so please be a good girl in the back seat and no fidgeting, no sickness, no little accidents. Did you go to the toilet before you left?"

I nodded vigorously. It was a lie. Sister Isobel had seemed already annoyed when she came to find me in my room and I hadn't wanted to make her worse by asking to use the bathroom. But there was no way on this earth I was prepared to go back inside the convent now for a wee.

I was out, and I was staying out. I would simply cross my legs and make the best of it. Besides, in my mind, I knew this journey off by heart. Hadn't I floated along these roads, time after time, in the dead of night, wearing nothing but my starchy nightdress? I knew how far it was and how long it would take.

* * *

It wasn't until the car left the convent gates that I suddenly clapped my hands over my mouth and shrieked.

"What about Freddie?" I gasped. "Where is my brother?"

All at once, I thought it was a trick, a set-up. I couldn't leave without him. Sister Isobel would know that. And so I would have to return, to rescue him, and she would pounce and keep me there for good. Was this all part of her wicked plan?

I could not go back. But I could not leave him there.

"I can't go without him," I said urgently. "Please."

The lady in the passenger seat was leafing through some papers on her knee.

"Yes, Freddie," she said eventually, tracing names down a list. "Sibling. 17.02.52. Yes…"

She trailed off and I was buzzing with panic, like I was plugged into an electric socket. The car was driving on – further and further away from the convent. I found myself in the ridiculous position of wanting it to turn around and go back.

But eventually, after licking her thumb and flicking over another page, she said: "Your brother Freddie has already left the convent. He will be at your home in fact, by the time you arrive."

I wasn't sure whether or not to believe her. I had trusted women like her before, believed I was going off on holiday, believed I was in for a treat.

But she turned and nodded and smiled kindly at me and I felt a little reassured.

"Freddie will be there," she repeated.

I had to admit to myself, too, that the social workers hadn't actually lied to me at all, on that fateful day. It wasn't them who made the story up about the holiday. It was my own father. I had done my best to block out that distressing truth, over the months and years.

But if Freddie was home already, that surely would mean that my family were ready for me and expecting me. That they wanted me. I was assured of a warm welcome.

The fields and hedges whizzed past and we went through towns and villages; places I didn't remember. In my mind's eye, I could see my six-year-old self, nose pressed against the window, brimming with a fatal mix of excitement and gullibility.

"Can you see the sea, Freddie?" I'd asked. "Shout if you see it first!"

Well, I was nine years old now, and still waiting.

We slowed as we reached Oldham, through the streets and the rat-runs, past the schools and the pubs. I didn't recognise it like I thought I would. But as we turned the corner into our council estate, the pressure in my chest was almost intolerable; my lungs were ready to pop. And then, there it was. The old green door, the falling down fence, the unloved scrap of garden out the front.

Home.

I wanted so much to jump out of the car and run inside. Yet I was strangely rooted to my seat, too. It was a funny mix: anxiety and shyness, joy and hysteria.

"Come along, Marie," said the social worker, opening the car door. "Surely you haven't forgotten which one is yours?"

She nodded to the row of houses with a smile. I climbed out, uncertain now, and stood behind her as she knocked on the door.

But then, from the other side, I heard my dad's voice, broad, sure, welcoming.

"That'll be her, that'll be our Mairin!"

And that was it. I heard my name, my own name, and the tension vanished like magic. I tumbled inside, half-intoxicated, and went into the living room, where Peter, Johnny and Jeanie were all waiting.

It was disconcerting for a moment. They stared at me, expectantly, as though they were waiting for a visitor. And that visitor was me. I didn't feel as though I could just plonk myself in the middle of them all. I had to wait for an invitation.

The little ones looked at me with interest and some suspicion, and I could see they didn't really remember me.

But Peter ventured: "Alright, Marie! You home for good now?"

He gave me a big smile and I felt my nerves loosen again. And then, there was Freddie, peering round the doorway, his face, as always, serious and giving little away.

"When did you get back?" I demanded.

"Yesterday," he said. "I came on my own. Boys and girls separate."

He shrugged as if to say he didn't understand it any more than I did. Dad had been talking to the social workers at the door, but he appeared next, his face split with a grin, his arms out wide.

"Come here," he said, and pulled me close. Mum came in from the kitchen, carrying a cute baby girl of about a year old in one arm – and a new baby boy in the other. Kathleen toddled along at the side of her and eyed me warily.

There was an awkward moment, when mum and I just looked at one another, rather bashfully. The silence, like the missing years, stretched between us.

"I've my hands full, with the little ones," she said in answer to the question nobody was asking.

And then, there was the sound of feet on the stairs and Christine bounded into the room and sidled, gloating, up to dad.

"You're back," she said nastily. "I stayed here, the whole time. You went away, but I was here."

There was a note of nauseating triumph in her voice and I burst into tears. Whatever I'd expected, it was not this. I had been usurped and cast aside by my own sister. She had clearly reigned supreme, on my throne, whilst I had been away. And now that I was here, she was refusing to give it back.

"Stop it now, stop it," dad was telling her. "You're being unkind."

But though Christine was silent, there was a glint in her eyes which said that this was far from over. That she was the right-hand man these days, and I would have a fight on my hands if I wanted my place back.

The tears flowed, until mum said to me: "Would you take Teresa for me, Mairin? I'm sure she'd like a cuddle with her big sister.

"I'm going to feed your new baby brother. We've called him Simon."

I was only too pleased to have the distraction and, with Teresa in my arms, I realised how foolish I had been to see this little girl as any kind of threat or replacement. She was beautiful, chubby cheeked and wide-eyed and I fell in love with her.

"I'm your big sis," I told her, as I tickled the creases in the back of her fat knees.

"And yours. And yours. And yours." I told the little faces next to me.

"Were you naughty, Marie?" Johnny asked. "Is that why you went away?"

It was a question I couldn't answer. Just like he couldn't answer why he'd been in the convent. I doubted he even remembered it at all.

There were a lot of bumps ahead. I couldn't possibly begin to see them all. But I was home, back in the fold, back where I belonged.

And that night, as I snuggled in the big bed with a Winifred doll on either side of me, Freddie and Peter to the left and Johnny, Jeanie and Christine to the right, I felt totally and absolutely content.

Chapter Nineteen

Peter's leg brace was propped up in the corner. Freddie was complaining I was taking up too much room. Little Johnny had his hand in mine.

I could hear mum in the next bedroom, singing Irish lullabies to Kathleen and Teresa. I had missed the sound of her voice so much. It almost hurt to listen to her songs.

Late that night, long after everyone was asleep, tears of sheer relief streamed down my face in the darkness. At last, I was home.

Chapter Twenty

Early the next morning, whilst my brothers and sisters, heavy and peaceful with sleep, snored around me, I woke to the sound of a phantom bell. For a moment, drowsy and confused. I was unsure where I was. Who I was.

"Kibby! Kibby!" screeched a voice in my head.

I pictured Dil and the big girls and everyone I had left behind, clutching their rosary beads and saying their prayers. I could see Sister Isobel, snapping out orders, the head honcho of suffering and abuse. I saw them plodding wearily down the corridor to collect their buckets and start the day's work.

And the tears came once more.

When I heard Teresa babbling and cooing in the next room, I was glad of the chance to get up and make myself useful. Lying in bed with nothing, absolutely nothing, to do, suddenly seemed ludicrous and lazy – unforgivably so.

And though she did not know me, Teresa met me with a big smile and I gathered her up into a cuddle and carried her off downstairs. There was bread for toast and milk to drink, and I made us both breakfast, cutting her toast into strips she could squeeze between her pudgy hands.

Looking around the old kitchen, now that my butterflies from yesterday had gone, I realised very little had changed.

From the rickety table, to the threadbare couch, and the half-empty cupboards, the hardship was ingrained.

But to me, poverty was like an old friend. A shabby old pair of slippers with holes in – no longer useful – but comfortable, familiar and smelling of home and acceptance.

There were a couple of family photos on the sideboard. One of me, Freddie and Peter, as toddlers. Another of mum with Kathleen. I thought back to my communion, and the photo of Freddie and me, but there was no sign of it.

I would have liked to have found it, if only to wipe the smile off Christine's face when she saw my beautiful dress and my bouquet. It was a churlish thought, but I was still smarting from her cruelty the day before.

The next footsteps on the bare floorboards upstairs were definitely my mother's. Though heavier than the kids, she was still very light on her feet. And I could hear her sighing and muttering a little too, in the bathroom.

For some funny reason, I felt a bit nervous. Like I had done something wrong and I was about to face up to it. She came into the kitchen, pulling an old house coat tight around her waist, and put a hand first on Teresa's cheek, and then mine.

"Did you sleep well in the old bed, Mairin?" she asked.

I nodded and smiled. I waited — expecting her to ask more. But that was it. I had been away for years, and she had nothing else at all that she wanted to know.

I was incredulous. She could have asked me so much; it was impossible to know where to start.

"Did you make any friends? What did they feed you? How did they treat you?"

Instead, there was nothing.

For my part, I had a string of painful questions. Questions I had rehearsed over and over in my head, night after night, in my lonely convent bed.

"Why was I sent there? Why me and not one of the others? What had I done wrong?"

But mum was busy now, lighting the stove, filling the kettle, getting breakfast ready. I couldn't open this box of snakes myself. I needed her help.

Most of all, I wanted her to ask me if the nuns were kind. Or not. I wanted her to give me the chance to tell her what had happened. The very worst of it. Still unsure exactly what *it* was, I knew it was wrong. And I didn't want to carry it around all alone.

I had needed my mum so many times over the years I was away. But now that I was home, I felt I needed her more than ever. Yet though we were in the same room, it seemed she was still as far off and inaccessible as before.

To a little girl, as I was then, my mum's reaction made me wonder whether she had really missed me after all. I was shocked, and probably a little put out, that she didn't want to know anything about my life for the past few years.

Only now, with hindsight, I can see that mum was almost as hurt and as damaged as I was. She was most likely too ashamed and distressed to talk about the reasons why she had sent her eldest daughter away. Or perhaps why I had been taken away from her.

And so, it went unsaid. Swept under the carpet without so much as an apology or even a regret. In the days to come I would wonder whether, in fact, I belonged here at all. I did not fit in at the convent. And now I did not fit in at home.

I was a stranger in the family. A cuckoo in the nest. A girl with no name.

* * *

The next day, it was back to business and I went to school along with Freddie, Peter, Christine, Johnny and Jeanie. I had to wear my convent clothes, because there were none for me at home. What little I'd had before leaving had been passed down to the younger ones. Besides, though I was small, they would no longer have fit me.

I had no choice but to wear my itchy jumper and my skirt.

"What are you wearing, Marie?" asked Christine, making no effort to disguise her distaste.

I hated the convent clothes. I felt as though they were unclean – infected. As though I was bringing the bad luck and the bad will from the convent into my family. Truth was that the convent clothes were better quality and better fitting than the ones my brothers and sisters were wearing. But I despised them all the same. I felt they were cursed.

"Can we go to the jumble sale, to see one-arm Rosie?" I asked mum. "I don't like these clothes. They're not mine."

But mum didn't commit herself. She had a familiar glazed look in her eyes, and she didn't seem to know exactly where she was or what was happening.

"Please?" I said. "I need some clothes, mum."

But she did not reply.

In the schoolyard, the local kids formed a scrum around me and Freddie.

"Where have you been? Where did you go?"

"Your Christine said you got sent away for being naughty."

"Your Peter said you'd gone off on holiday."

I said nothing. I didn't want to tell them anything. Shame. Trauma. Pride. Whatever it was, I just kept it all inside.

In the days afterwards, I was determined to be happy. I was so grateful, so pitifully thankful to be home, and I thought it would be easy to just fit right back in where I had left off, to slot into the old, familiar routine, as though I had never been away.

But I was wrong.

The shadow of the anguish I had suffered was hanging over me, bearing down on me. Sometimes I felt suffocated, strangulated. I could barely breathe. It was impossible to shrug off the years of regimented pain and simply melt back into family life.

I could feel the attacks from the coat-hangers. I could see the water splashing into the enormous washroom sinks. I could hear the lumpy porridge splatting into the bowls.

I could not escape.

Dad noticed something was wrong. Like mum, he never once mentioned the convent. But he would say, "Come here, our Mairin, sit by me."

We would sit for hours with him chatting easily, no doubt hoping that I might confide in him. Or perhaps he was terrified of me opening up. Maybe he couldn't have coped with the truth.

But I would not and could not tell him anything. The words just did not come. I felt a little like I was a miniature war veteran. As though I had just come home from battle and I was weary and traumatised. Like everyone around me had been briefed:

"Don't ask her. Don't ask her what she did there. She can't handle it. Just don't mention the convent."

And Sister Isobel was the bogeyman in the corner. An infestation, a cancer, a curse. She was the black crow in the eaves, the elephant in the room and nobody dared even speak her name.

So when dad met me on the street after school and asked:

"How are you, Mairin? How are you settling back in?"

I would reply:

"Smashing thanks, dad!"

It was a lie. But it was the best I could do.

Besides, I knew that my parents had enough to worry about. They were as painfully poor as ever. There were nine children now and Freddie, the eldest, was still just ten years old. Mum seemed worryingly volatile and unpredictable. Her moods swung from one extreme to another and any peace in the house was fragile and temporary.

One evening, I was sewing from a small kit, by the fire, and she and dad were arguing because she had run out of money and dad hadn't earned anything that week. It was so dismally commonplace an argument, that me and my brothers and sisters were bored by this sort of thing. They were jammed in the same old rut.

Mum became more and more agitated until she was screaming at the top of her voice.

"Just go!" she yelled at my dad. "Go and never come back!"

Dad spun around in frustration and grabbed the needlework out of my hand. I screeched in protest as he tossed it into the fire, and it melted and vanished in the flames within a few moments.

I was more shocked than upset. It was the first and only time I had ever seen my father lose his temper and I realised that the stress was becoming unbearable for him, too.

No, it was not fair for me to burden them further with my trauma.

I worried, too, that if I became a problem at home, I might have to go back to a convent. My siblings' words went round and round in my head:

"Have you been naughty, Marie? Is that why you went away?"

What if that was true? What if I set one foot out of line and they sent me away? In calmer moments, I knew it was nonsense. But I'd have panicky thoughts, in the middle of the night, where it seemed like a possibility.

It had happened once. It could happen again.

I wished away the years in my head, hoping for a fast-forward button that I could press and make myself grown-up – in an instant! I wanted to be too old to be sent back to a convent. I wanted to be safe.

But there was no time machine.

So instead, I resolved to do my best to be good. At home, I tried to make myself indispensable. When Simon cried during the night, I would bound out of bed to rock him back to sleep. I helped with the nappies and the feeds for the babies. I took the little ones to school, their hands in mine. I told them bedtime stories and sang nursery rhymes.

My favourite, and dad's, was *Daisy, Daisy, Give Me Your Answer Do*. Early in the mornings, I'd take the milk tokens and a big bag and buy seven bottles of milk from the local shop. The bag was so heavy I had to drag it back, being careful not to crack the bottles on the way.

In the afternoons, after school, I'd take the pram out and collect wood for the fires. I'd often take two or three of the little ones with me, too, to give mum a break.

"You're a good girl, Mairin. You're my right-hand man," dad smiled.

I could feel Christine scowling behind my back, but I glowed with pride. It felt like a double victory; earning dad's praise and displacing her, all at the same time.

Hearing my parents pay me compliments was addictive. I had missed more than three years of parenting, and in many ways I was still that frightened six-year-old girl who had left home one day to go away on holiday. I needed reassurance and reinforcement, every day. Just a word from mum or a cuddle from dad was enough.

Yet in other ways, I was more self-sufficient and grown up than many kids my age. I enjoyed responsibility, I always had.

Some days, I was like a middle-aged woman, worrying about what the kids would eat for tea and whether there were enough clean pairs of socks for the following morning. Other times, all I wanted to do was curl up on my mother's knee with Winifred, and cry myself to sleep. The two aspects of my character rubbed along uneasily and in opposition.

And I also knew that sometimes I was probably trying *too* hard. I could be overbearing in my efforts to impress and ingratiate myself back into the fold. I was like an unwanted duckling, pecking at the nest to be let back in.

Chapter Twenty

"Let me change the baby's nappy," I insisted. "No, I'll go to the shops. I can bring the wood. I can do it on my own."

I felt as though I had to prove myself. And yet I also needed them to prove themselves to me. I was a ball of conflict and contradiction. But I threw my efforts into being a surrogate mum, a home help and an all round right-hand man.

While at school, I was more hard-working and attentive than I had ever been. I was doing well in class and my teacher was impressed.

"You're making good progress, Marie," she said. "I'm pleased with you."

Again, the words of praise were like droplets of gold to a little girl who had been starved of attention for so long.

I was thankful just to have a name.

Chapter Twenty One

But just as I hoped I might be getting used to my old surroundings again, dad announced we were moving house. He had never really liked living at Second Avenue. It was part of an overspill estate, houses thrown up by the council to ship the poorest out of town and out of sight.

But my dad had always loved living in the town centre and he missed the old communities and the hustle and bustle.

"We're going back!" he announced.

The move was exciting. All we thought about was finding new dens, new hills to sledge down, new places for hide and seek.

Our next house, at New Radcliffe Street, was a little bigger than the last. But the toilet was outside, down a set of steps, and into the back garden. And though there were three bedrooms again, we had two big beds in one room, and the others lay empty.

"We can't afford to light a fire in every room," dad told me. "So it makes sense for us all to pile in together. Just for now.

"We'll soon have enough money for a fire in every bedroom."

I hugged my shoulders together, smiling just at the thought of it. I'd had years of sleeping in my own lonely bed and I knew the misery it brought. This way was much better.

For a couple of days, we worked hard to get the new house up to scratch. Us older kids helped dad to carry furniture and unpack boxes.

As a rag and bone man, dad gave out donkey stones – scrubbing stones – in exchange for old clothes, and so he always had a plentiful supply. He handed Christine and I a stone each and we scrubbed at the doorsteps and the window sills until the place looked shipshape.

As I scrubbed, I had a horrible flashback to my six-year-old self, kneeling on the wooden floors at the convent, scrubbing until my fingers bled. Every time I lifted my head I expected to see Sister Isobel's clackety shoes in my eye-line.

"No," I muttered to myself. "Stop it, Marie, stop it!"

Christine was kneeling next to me and she giggled in amusement.

"Talking to yourself now," she said. "You're going mad!"

I tried to ignore her and I continued to scrub. Nobody noticed I was an expert. Nobody asked me where I had learned to clean so efficiently.

But whilst everyone else was busy and carried away with the mood, I saw mum, standing back, isolated and almost removed from the scene. She seemed vacant, sullen sometimes. And yet I knew that wasn't the real her. I worried for her.

When the unpacking was done, it was time to go back to school.

"It's a long way to school from here," I suddenly realised. "How are we going to get there?"

"You're going to a new school," dad told us. "It's just around the corner."

It was a disappointment. I would miss my old school. But then, I had my brothers and sisters to keep me company, and so I wasn't too upset, either.

Our new school, St Mary's, was a Catholic primary, and it was just a case of going out of the back door, across a small road, and into the school yard.

"Think of the lie in every morning," dad pointed out. "We're so close to the new school."

That first day was bitterly cold. I had Kathleen on one side of me, and Jeanie on the other. But as we walked into the school hall, I suddenly froze. There, directing children, was a woman in a veil with a long, black habit. A nun.

My heart stopped. For a terrifying moment, I thought it was Sister Isobel and that she had followed me here, as a trick. It was beyond terrifying.

I gripped my sisters' hands, cold sweat trickling down my back, my heart now racing. I stood, rooted to the spot, expecting her to swivel around and scream: "Come here, Kibby! You are a Child Of God!"

"What's the matter, Marie?" asked Jeanie.

My mouth opened and closed again but I said nothing. And then, the nun turned to us and smiled and said: "You must be the Kibblewhites. Come along girls, don't stand there gawping."

The relief that she was not Sister Isobel, after all, was overwhelming. I felt close to tears, but I swallowed them back, knowing I had to make a good impression.

Not only was the headmistress a nun, but my own class teacher was, too. I reminded myself that I did not live here, and that they could not control me and abuse me as had happened before.

I had to be strong, for my little sisters. But it was hard.

Just a swish of the habit and I could hear Sister Isobel clack-clacking down the corridor towards me. I felt her breath on my neck as she leered over me with the egg in the cup. I could even taste the snotty, lumpy mixture inside.

"Marie! Are you paying attention?" asked my new teacher, and I nodded feverishly.

The flashbacks and the memories plagued me, day after day. When we closed our eyes to pray in school, I felt as though I was back there, with Dil at my side, anxiously clasping my rosary beads like my life depended on it.

But I learned, as the weeks went on, that the nuns, though strict, were fair. I could never have brought myself to trust them. But I did not fear them, either.

There were some mornings when I overslept a little or I couldn't find a hairbrush for the girls' ponytails or there was no milk in for breakfast. It was inevitable that occasionally we would arrive late at school. One morning, as we hurried in after the bell had rung, the headmistress poked her head out of her office and said:

"Late again, Kibblewhites! What's the excuse today?"

My legs turned to jelly.

"Our alarm clock didn't go off, Sister, I'm sorry," I stuttered. "I really am."

We didn't even have an alarm clock. That was the real problem. But I couldn't tell her that. There were a few moments of silence, while we waited, breathless, for our punishment.

And then she said: "Don't let it happen again, girls," and she went back to her work.

It was a huge anti-climax and it was several more seconds before I realised we were off the hook and we could go. The little ones were tugging at my hands, pulling me along.

As the weeks went on, I learned that the very worst punishment from the nuns was a rap on the outstretched hand with a ruler. Several of my friends had been given the ruler and assured me that it wasn't so bad after all.

"Just pull your jumper over the end of your fingers and it softens the smack," they told me.

I smiled. The ruler did not frighten me. Not after what I had been through. Even so, I made sure I was never in trouble. I could not take the risk.

Chapter Twenty One

Bonfire Night 1962 was coming and in the build up, we were industrious and busy, as always. We approached the night with military precision, collecting wood and hiding it in a disused shed. We took it in turns to stand guard and keep a look out for enemy attacks.

Bonfires were a serious business.

The night arrived and the air was thick with smoke and mischief. Wayward rockets whistled past our ears. Kids had battles with bangers. And our bonfire, the biggest and the brightest, burned all night long.

And it wasn't just the bonfire that made me feel warm inside. I couldn't begin to explain, nor did I want to, what it meant to me to be at home this time.

But there was an uneasy feeling too, that I was forcing it, papering over the cracks and pretending that everything was fine. Because as I watched the guy, burning and disintegrating, his head lolling and falling into the flames, I felt empty and anxious. I painted on a smile and I screamed at the stray fireworks, just like everyone else.

But in my mind's eye, I could see Dil, writing words in the darkness with her sparkler. I could hear Sister Isobel:

"Get Kibby, get Kibby."

The memories were seared on my brain. I was a branded like a slave. Tainted by it. And suddenly I shivered. All the warmth was gone.

I was home from the convent. But a part of me was stuck back there. And I wondered if it always would be so.

* * *

It was one lunchtime, in the school playground, that a girl called Marion, from my class, announced that she wanted to fight me – because I was the new girl. In school, so far, I had kept myself to myself, I had kept my head down. And my silence had been mistaken for arrogance.

"Come on then," Marion said, weighing me up, and jutting out her chin. "How about it?"

And though I didn't like fighting – I was much too small to be any good at it – the thought didn't frighten me, either. I'd had so many beatings at the convent, I had stared true misery in the face, day after day. And nothing, I reasoned, could be worse than that. Certainly nothing this scrawny girl could dole out, that was for sure.

"Yeah, no problem," I retorted. "Four o'clock. School gates."

Word went around the school and soon the other kids were calling it The Greatest Show On Earth. We might as well have sold tickets.

After school, we met at the gates, with a huge, expectant cluster around us. Kathleen was clinging to me, too small to enjoy it, and too scared to leave my side.

In all the chaos, she was jostled by a gang of boys and she banged her head on a wall and began to cry.

In that moment, I snapped. It was just like being back at the convent, seeing the big boy push Freddie. Or hearing

Johnny crying in the nursery. I could not bear to see one of my siblings hurt.

I marched over to Marion, my temper blazing, and flung a right hook.

"Don't bring my sister into this!" I yelled.

We went at it, pulling hair and throwing punches, until a car pulled up and a woman stuck her head out of the driver's window.

"Stop that now!" she shouted. "I'll report you both to your teachers."

I was worried about getting into trouble, in case my parents heard of it, and so I backed off. The lads in the crowd were keen for the fight to continue on waste ground elsewhere, but I had done and said enough.

"Come on," I said to Kathleen, glaring at Marion. "We're off home."

The next morning… Marion was waiting at the school gates.

She smiled at me and we walked into class together, linking arms. From that moment, we were inseparable.

We became best friends and soul-mates and I loved her like a sister.

Chapter Twenty Two

The following year, Mum fell pregnant with her tenth child and in November 1963, she gave birth to a beautiful little girl, Denise.

"Every child is a gift from God," Mum told me, as she wrapped her new daughter – her sixth – in the same shawl she had used for all ten of her children.

"A gift from God."

I nodded but deep down, I felt uncomfortable at the idea that my siblings were, in some way, presents from God. Sister Isobel had been at pains to point out on a daily basis that I was a Child of God, and it had felt more of a malignancy, a chronic illness, than a blessing.

I wasn't sure I wanted the same for my brothers and sisters.

And if God sent babies as presents, why didn't he send clothes and food and money for coal as well? It didn't make sense. I was beginning to wonder how many Gods there were because some of them definitely didn't seem to be on our side.

Chapter Twenty Two

In the evenings, kneeling with my siblings at the side of the bed, I would pray, quietly but passionately, for help to come. I prayed that the God in charge of poverty, whoever he was, would take pity on our family and send us good luck.

But until that time, we were relying on my dad.

"You will have to go out with the cart, Fred," mum told him. "I have Mairin to help me at home. You need to go out and earn.

"We've ten mouths to feed now."

Dad seemed to age visibly as she spoke. He nodded but then he said:

"There's no money to be earned in November, the weather has been foul. We'll have to make do with what we can."

In the evenings, though, he would quite often say to me:

"Hold the fort here, Mairin, I'm off on business."

I felt pleased that he was out working. This was surely a good sign. But when he came back from his 'business' I noticed he was sometimes carrying a bottle of ale. Other times, he would bring back a couple of packets of 'salt n shake' crisps for us to share.

And it was with a sinking heart that I realised dad's business was down at the local pub. And instead of earning money, he was spending it.

Looking back, I can hardly blame him for wanting to escape his reality for a while.

We were packed like sardines, even in bed, and the house was a constant hub of noise. There were babies screaming and crying, little ones shouting or giggling, almost all the time. Sometimes, I'd catch mum sitting on a chair with her hands pressed tightly over her ears.

"Come on, Kathleen," dad would say, half-confused, half-exasperated.

He didn't understand post-natal depression. None of us did. I don't think mum ever even saw a doctor. But I do know that her life was miserable and, try as she might, she could not bring herself to enjoy the many children she loved so much.

Christmas came and I loved throwing myself into the old traditions: putting on a nativity play, singing carols, dividing up the little gifts we got from charity workers.

I had missed it all so much. And I was determined not to complain when the gifts were not wrapped. I did not allow myself to feel sad that there was no Christmas tree and no Christmas cake.

I was with my family and I was determined to be thankful – at Christmas, more than ever before.

* * *

In September 1964, aged 11, I went off to high school, with Marion, my partner in crime, by my side. It was a quick growing-up process and at lunchtimes, we found ourselves in playground cliques with older girls.

"Ever kissed a boy, Marie?" one of them asked. "Ever had a boyfriend?"

It was an innocent enough question, light-hearted and friendly. But it punctured my heart. I had an alarming, 90mph flashback to my convent bed, a moist mouth on mine, a tongue pushing so hard that I was almost swallowing my own.

"I will show you how to French-kiss a boy," whispered a silky smooth voice in my head.

I shuddered as the bile rose in my throat.

"What's up, Marie?"

It was Marion, her hand on my coat sleeve.

"You look white as a sheet. Are you going to be sick?"

I shook my head, fighting desperately to shut out the vision. The fingers like tentacles. The lips. The ice-cold horror.

"I'm fine," I insisted. "I'm OK, really."

But that night, it played round and round, on a loop, in my head. And I realised, for the first time, that what the big girls had done to me at the convent was sexual. I began to make the link between what adults did in bed, and what they had done to me. And yet I was just a child.

It was a sickening and mind-blowing epiphany.

I tried hard to bury it, to push it down deeper and deeper into my subconscious. I thought that by planting layer upon layer of happy memories, I could somehow squeeze out all the bad ones. Like there would be no space left in my mind.

But it got worse, not better.

My friends got boyfriends. They had posters of pop-stars they fancied. Elvis and Cliff Richard.

"What do you think, Marie?" Marion asked me. "Would you French kiss him?"

The phrase turned my stomach. It was all I could do not to scream.

"No," I replied flatly. "I don't like any of them. I don't want a boyfriend and I'm never getting married and that's that."

* * *

Freddie, in his own way, struggled even more than I did to adjust to life back home. Like a grizzled veteran of Vietnam, he walked around with empty eyes and a blank stare.

At school, he got into lots of trouble. He was always in fights, and before long he was the undisputed cock of the school. He would fight anyone – anywhere. Like me, he had no fear of physical violence. Ironically, it had been knocked out of us both at the convent.

I realised, much later, that aggression was Freddie's coping mechanism.

But as a little girl, anxious not to cause any problems, desperate to hang on to my place in the family, I saw him as a troublemaker. And I kept my distance.

It was sad, after all we had been through. But Freddie and I were no longer close by the time we came home. We were sent to different high schools and I saw less and less of him. But his fights were legendary and I usually heard about them, third and fourth hand, from my friends.

"Your Freddie is something else," they whistled. "He can batter anyone he likes."

They were filled with admiration, as kids are. But I felt a terrible, dull sadness. I didn't know the details of what had happened to Freddie at the convent. But I knew he had been damaged and all but destroyed by the regime, just as I had. Yet we couldn't even bring ourselves to say it out loud.

We had suffered along parallel paths and there was no crossroads, no meeting point, for either of us.

A catharsis, if and when it ever came, would be a solitary one.

* * *

As we hit our teenage years Marion and I became closer still. And there were times when I desperately wanted to confide in her, to share my anguish with her.

But there was never a right time. And she knew me well enough not to force the issue. Deep down, I still carried a keen sense of shame and humiliation. As though it could somehow have been my fault.

I was worried, too, that if word got out there would be some people who would dine out on my suffering. I had seen a glimpse of that with Christine. The way she almost enjoyed seeing me squirm. Or at least, that was how I saw it. It seemed best, all round, not to rip open old wounds.

And so I clutched my secret to me, like an armoured shield, believing that if nobody knew about it, it might eventually go away. Instead of dwelling on the past, I tried to push myself, forcefully, into the future.

"When we leave school, we could get a flat together," Marion said to me. "Nice little place, handy for town.

"We could have our own drinks cabinet and a colour telly!"

We laughed and laughed. It sounded like decadence gone mad. But it was a nice idea.

"Seriously, though, we should definitely save up for a flat, as soon as we get jobs," she said.

I nodded in agreement. It sounded fantastic. But I thought of all the little ones back home. And I knew it would never happen. I couldn't abandon them. My face fell and Marion gave me a dig in the ribs.

"Cheer up!" she laughed. "We'll get a black and white telly instead if it means that much to you!"

Some of the girls in our group began seeing boyfriends. One girl, Carol, had an older boyfriend who drove a motorbike. He'd pick her up from school and take her to a pub outside town, where they served under-aged drinkers.

"You should come with us, Marie," she told me. "It's such a laugh, honestly. You should get yourself a boyfriend and let your hair down a bit."

She was just trying to be friendly. But I smiled and shook my head.

"Not my thing," I told her.

But I could never tell her why.

* * *

At 15, and before our final exams had started, Marion decided to leave school and get a job. But my teachers had selected me to stay on and finish my studies.

"We think you're going to do well in your exams, Marie," they told me. "We'd like you to work hard and give it your best shot."

I was pleased with myself. But when I went home, to tell my parents, I could see the worry in their eyes.

"We were thinking you would get a job, like Freddie, and help with the bills," dad explained. "But if you want to stay at school, it's up to you."

I wasn't sure what to do. I enjoyed my studies. But I had to look after my family, I knew that.

My headmaster, Mr Marsden, spoke to my parents and begged them to support me. Even the local priest from our parish church, St Patrick's, got involved.

He helped my parents to apply for a grant, and a cheque arrived in the post. We had never even seen a cheque before and my dad danced around the living room with it like it was made of solid silver.

I was thrilled, thinking the money would see me through my exams and until I left school. But only weeks later, the money was all gone. And we were struggling once again.

"I can't carry on at school," I decided. "It's just not fair."

I wanted mum or dad to say to me: "Don't leave school. Finish your exams. Think of yourself Mairin, just this once."

I prayed that they would step in. That's all it would have taken. But they didn't say it. And I knew they never would.

It wasn't long to my first written exams, and my teacher was horrified when I made the announcement. But my mind was made up. And so, before my 16th birthday, I left school; with dreams I would never realise and potential I would never fulfil. I had wanted to train as a nurse, I had hoped to make a difference. Instead, I found a job at a local bakery and worked hard, giving every penny of my weekly cash wage to my parents.

Working on the sausage roll line at the bakery was its own education – in swearing and filthy jokes. My parents had never sworn at home and it was both shocking and hilarious for me.

"I won't have that type of language under my roof," dad warned me.

But at work, amongst my pals, the air was blue. My time was taken up working long shifts at the bakery, 7.30am – 4pm, and over-time if I could get it. And every evening, I was busy helping out at home; washing, ironing and cooking. Looking after the little ones. Helping the bigger ones with homework. I had no time for anything else.

I earned eight pounds a week and gave the lot to my parents.

Mum's depression seemed worse, if anything, as time went on. One day, when I came home from work, dad met me in the street, agitated and upset.

"Your mum has had a bad turn," he told me. "We had a nun call at the house and your mum attacked her."

I gasped in shock.

Dad explained the nun, from the children's school, had become concerned at mum's behaviour and had tried to take Denise from her arms.

"Your mother flew at her like a wildcat," dad told me, shaking his head in disbelief. "She pulled her veil right off. She had to be dragged away. What a mess. What an embarrassment."

Instantly, I thought of the convent. I thought of how the nuns had previously taken away three of mum's babies. And I could understand that, fearing it might happen again, she had lost all control.

She had thought lightning was going to strike again.

Even so, it was hard to mitigate for such outrageous behaviour. She was the talk of the whole street. Most people didn't even dare make eye contact with nuns, never mind wrestle them to the ground. But for me, it was another sign that mum was ill, it was another cry for help.

I felt anxious around her, anxious for her. She was a ticking timebomb and I worried what she might do next. It was another trigger for me to take more responsibility away from her, and onto myself.

One day, mum was reading the local paper and she said: "Mairin, you won't believe this, Marion is in the newspaper."

I hadn't seen Marion for a good few months since I started work at the bakery; I'd just been too busy.

"What's she done?" I asked.

I thought maybe she'd won a competition.

"She's dead," mum replied flatly. "Brain tumour."

The world spun around me. My knees gave way and I felt myself sink to the floor. She was only 17, like me. We'd had so many dreams and plans. Hers had been snuffed out. And mine, without my best friend, seemed dull and grey and pointless.

Chapter Twenty Three

I was still only 17 when I met my first boyfriend, Bill Foster. I was walking home after a late shift, when I recognised two girls from the bakery.

"We're nipping in the pub for half a lager and black," said one. "Fancy joining us, Marie?"

I hesitated. I had never been in a pub before. And I knew I really should get home.

"Go on," said the other one. "We won't be long. Just a quick one."

And so I followed them in. I ordered half a lager and lime – my first ever. Next to the jukebox I noticed a young bloke, shirt unbuttoned, with a tattoo showing.

As we sat down with our drinks, he got up and walked towards us, and the girls I was with both giggled and blushed. He introduced himself as Bill and we chatted for a while. I learned that he was three years older than me and worked on the buses.

After my drink was finished, I made my excuses, and left the pub. To my surprise, he followed.

"I'd like to walk you home, if you don't mind," he said.

I wasn't sure.

"Just to the top of my street," I told him. "Any further and my dad might see you. And then you're for it."

I didn't feel comfortable walking with him. I didn't like the thought of walking with any man. And at the top of the street, as we said goodnight, he leaned in and slipped a bracelet off my wrist.

"You'll have to meet me tomorrow night, now," he said with a smile. "Or you can't have your bracelet back."

I wasn't sure I wanted to see him again. I didn't want or need a boyfriend. And it wasn't that I was particularly fond of the bracelet, more that I didn't like the idea of him keeping something of mine.

"Tomorrow night," I agreed.

We went to a pub in town. Bill wanted The Rolling Stones on the jukebox. I wanted Elvis. It was our first difference of opinion, and the first of many.

"I don't want a boyfriend," I told him again.

But Bill didn't take no for an answer. And somehow, we ended up going out. He would wait for me outside the bakery, to walk me home. And though I had no money of my own, he'd treat me to new clothes and take me out. He gave me a cute little cigarette lighter too which I loved; we both smoked back then.

"I love you," he told me with a smile.

But as our relationship moved on, Bill wanted more. The first time he tried to kiss me, on the mouth, I pulled back, disgusted. I was haunted by images of the big girls at the convent, of the starchy bed and the wooden hangers.

"I can't do this," I gasped, retching with the shock.

But Bill persevered.

On our next date, he gave me a record, *Let's Spend the Night Together* by The Rolling Stones. I responded by buying him *Give Me Just a Little More Time*. It was old-fashioned texting I suppose, flirting without words. We fell in love over music, Bill converted me into a Rolling Stones fan, I got him listening to the Eagles and to Helen Shapiro.

But eventually, I ran out of a little more time, and the crunch came.

I couldn't tell Bill about the abuse. And so I had to go along with him. But the truth was, I hated any kind of intimacy. To me, sex was violence. Sex was fear. Sex was pain. I gritted my teeth and got through it, because that was how it was for me. Bill couldn't have known, he was just a young man.

I saw my GP, who was a devout Catholic, and asked him for the contraceptive pill. I didn't want ten children, one after another, like my mother had. But he just tutted at me and shook his head in weary disapproval.

"You need to concentrate on your studies," he told me. "Forget about boyfriends and run along now."

One year on, in September 1971, Bill and I were married. I wore a satin lilac hot pant suit for the ceremony at

Oldham Register Office. Afterwards, we went for a burger at the Wimpy bar next door.

If I was honest, I didn't really want to get married. But it was a way of showing my mum and dad that I was settling down and becoming an adult. For me, marriage was respectability. And I was fond of Bill, too. He seemed to love me, which counted for a lot.

Now that we were officially a couple, I took the plunge and decided to try to tell him about the convent. I wasn't sure how much I could verbalise, but I hoped, by sharing the weight, that it might lessen the strain. My heart hammered as I opened my mouth. It was a huge moment for me. But I didn't get past the first few words when he said abruptly:

"Don't tell me this. Tell your father."

And that was that. Subject closed. Maybe he was embarrassed or frightened by the enormity of it. Perhaps he wasn't interested. I would never know.

* * *

Bill and I rented a terraced house, near to my family home, so that I could go back each day to help. And one morning, when I went home, I spotted my lighter, my gift from Bill, on the mantlepiece.

"I've been looking everywhere for that!" I exclaimed.

"I think Christine took a fancy to it," my dad replied. "Why not let her have it?"

Chapter Twenty Three

I was furious. There she was again, coveting what was mine. If she couldn't have my place in the family, she wanted my lighter. Or that's how it seemed to me. And it didn't stop there. I found a new dress of mine in her wardrobe. Then a pair of shoes. We didn't have the sort of relationship where we could borrow each other's clothes without asking. I saw this as an act of spite. Of ownership. And I wasn't standing for it. I waited in the living room for Christine to come home, and then we had it out.

"You're just jealous of me, you always have been," I told her.

She smirked and in a flash I was nine years old and she was sidling up to dad, looking down her nose at me.

"I stayed and you got sent away…"

I lunged at her, grabbing a handful of hair, and we fell to the floor, grappling and fighting.

"Leave me alone!" I yelled.

And I marched from the house, my blood boiling, but with my lighter and my clothes left behind. Doubtless this would not have been such a big deal, if I hadn't ever been sent away. Poor Christine was suffering because of the convent, and she had never even been near the place.

Early in 1972, I discovered I was pregnant and I was over the moon. I had grown up around babies, I had been a little mother since I was no more than a toddler myself.

And now, this was my chance to do it for real.

The pregnancy went like a dream, and in September 1972, our son, Shane, was born. I adored him. And as I held him in my arms, I knew in that moment that nobody – nuns, priests or high up deity, would ever snatch him from me. I would protect him with every breath in my body.

He was a beautiful, happy little boy.

Mum came to see him in hospital, bringing with her a bottle of Guinness for me, and she beamed as she held him in her arms.

"My first grandchild," she said proudly.

But that December, aged three months, Shane picked up a cold. He grizzled for a few days over Christmas but I felt sure he'd come through it. But on the morning of December 29, Bill got out of bed early and cried out: "Marie! He's not breathing! The baby's dead!"

I didn't believe him for a moment. I dived out of bed, over to the cot and peered at my son. He was a deathly pale, almost bluish-grey. And his tiny hands were clenched, in fists.

When I touched him, his skin was icy cold.

There was a horrible, heart-rending scream, and I realised the voice was mine. Bill steered me outside, to a motor garage next door, and asked the owner to look after me.

"Keep her safe," he pleaded. "I need to call an ambulance for our son."

From the office of the garage, I watched as my baby son, the most precious love I had ever known, was carried from our home in a red blanket.

"They will bring him home," I repeated, over and over. "They will bring him home."

But the hours passed and baby Shane did not return. Doctors told us he had suffered a cot death. My poor heart was smashed into pieces.

The gods had taken him, after all. I had sworn that nobody would touch a hair on his head. Yet somehow, they had stolen him from me anyway.

For weeks, I was blindsided by grief. I went through life on auto-pilot, pining for my darling baby boy. Bill grieved differently. As a man, in those days, he was expected to be strong. But inside, I imagine he was crumbling, just as I was.

It was only the realisation that I was pregnant again, three months on, that made me snap back to reality.

"You have to look after yourself, you're carrying a new life," Bill told me. "We have to look to the future, focus on the new baby."

I knew he was right. But there was more tragedy around the corner. Mum had not been eating well for months and Dad eventually insisted she went into hospital for tests. The results, when they came, were devastating.

Mum had advanced stomach cancer and had only a few months left to live. After losing Shane, I was numb. I could barely take the news in. We carried her bed downstairs and I helped care for her at home. It was hardest for Simon and Denise, they were still so little, and too young to lose a parent.

In April 1973, mum took her final breath, aged just 42.

Kathleen came running to my house with the news. Together we stumbled back to the family home, blinded by our tears, clinging to each other for comfort.

Our lovely Irish mother was gone.

I missed her terribly. But I also mourned the life she hadn't had, the things she had missed out on. Much of her life had been filled with sadness and despair. I wished it could have been different. She was a woman with ten children who probably never had a moment to herself for many years. And yet, I think she was lonely and alone, much of the time.

With mum gone, I had to take on even more tasks at home. Dad struggled, especially with the younger ones. Teresa was eleven years old, Simon was ten, and Denise was only nine. I would go home each morning to get them up for school, make the breakfasts and get the uniforms ready. In the afternoons, I would be there to meet them at the school gates.

In August 1973, I gave birth to a little boy weighing a bouncing 9lbs. It was bittersweet. He was a handsome little cherub, perfect in every way, but he reminded me so much of his big brother and I couldn't help thinking of what could, what should, have been.

"Let's call him Shane," Bill suggested.

But I wouldn't hear of it.

"This isn't Shane. We will never get Shane back," I told him.

We would never fully get over losing our son, and my heart went out to Bill. He ached, as I did, to have Shane back in his arms. But this was not the way.

In the end, we agreed to name our new son Lee.

I was neurotically overprotective, and hardly slept as I watched over him, day and night. For six months, I slept with him on my chest, so that I could hear him breathing.

But despite my worries, he grew and thrived and I was so thankful.

I can understand, during that period, that Bill possibly felt pushed out and side-lined. I was so busy with my baby – my beautiful baby – that I had no time for him. And I did not even try to pretend otherwise.

The following August, I gave birth to twins. A boy, and a girl. With two babies at once, I felt blessed, as though one was a gift from Shane.

But now I really had my hands full.

Lee was only a year old, so I had three babies of my own to look after, and I still had all my siblings under my wing, too.

At one time, one or more of my brothers and sisters – except for Christine – came to live with me. Peter stayed for a time. Johnny did, too. And I welcomed them like a mother hen, bringing her chicks home to roost. It was more than sisterly love, I had a matriarchal duty to them. It was a sense of obligation I'd had almost since I was in the womb.

But whilst I was as close as ever to my siblings, I had huge cracks appearing in my marriage and Bill and I argued a lot.

He didn't like me visiting my dad every day, he wanted me at home, with him.

"Well, that's tough," I replied. "I'll do as I like."

As a child, I had been bullied and persecuted and terrorised to within an inch of my sanity. So now it was time to stand up for myself, as I saw it. Our rows became more frequent, but I dug my heels in. I shouted just as loud, and sometimes louder. And I saw it as a huge step forward.

Back then, I congratulated myself on being forward-thinking and progressive.

Yet at the same time, I was determined to stick it out, in a marriage where we both were miserable, for the sake of our children. It did not for a moment occur to me that I ought to leave.

Clearly, as I look back now, I realise I was taking much smaller steps towards emancipation than I had thought. And I was going in completely the wrong direction too.

As time passed, I began to remind myself of my own mother. A baby on each arm, a pram to push, and children playing around me. I was exhausted, harassed and constantly scraping around for money.

And so, at 23 years of age, I made a huge decision. I wanted my sense of self back again. I wanted some free time and some control over my own body. I made up my mind to be sterilised.

The reason I had been sent to the convent, I now understood, was poverty. Abject poverty. It had all started, and ended, with poverty. Too many children and not enough money. Plain and simple. My mother's depression had been caused, or at the very least exacerbated, by having too many children in too short a space of time, with too little money to care for them.

Roman Catholics were forbidden by the church to use contraception and every child, however unwanted and unbudgeted for, was a gift from God. And so when their families spilled over it was, of course, the church who stepped in and took the extra ones away.

I was determined that the same thing was not going to happen in my family.

It was a vicious and rotten circle and I was going to be the one to square it. Much as I loved my mother, I did not want to be like her. I had to break the cycle.

The convent was still shaping my life, overshadowing my thoughts, influencing every decision I made. But this one, I felt, was for the best. I had been controlled and coerced all my life and this was a way of freeing myself. Of putting my foot down.

On the night before my op, I calmly broke the news to Bill.

"Can you look after the children tomorrow?" I asked him. "Only I'm going into hospital, to have my tubes tied."

I had expected a row or even a fight. But I got neither. Bill simply raised his eyebrows and said nothing. Was I expecting too much of him? Or even too little? Looking back now, my behaviour seems unreasonable. Cruel even. But I was driven by a need to not to repeat the mistakes of the past at all costs.

At the hospital the next morning, the obstetrician did her best to talk me out of it.

"You're far too young," she told me. "You'll change your mind. You'll want more children."

But I shook my head.

"I won't," I insisted. "I'm looking forward to being sterilised. I love my children, but I don't want any more."

When I came round from the surgery, I was sore but triumphant. I felt like I was taking back control. Like I had got myself back.

Chapter Twenty Four

Whilst my mum had possibly struggled to bond with her children, I had over bonded. I felt every emotion that they did. Every pain, every disappointment, every triumph, and it was magnified a million times over.

It was a struggle to keep my maternal instincts in check.

Lee had hardly any hair, save a few wisps, as a baby, but then as a toddler, he grew a mop of blonde curls. One day, he had been playing with some little girls across the street, and when he came back indoors, I gasped in shock.

"Who did that?" I demanded. "Who did that to my baby boy?"

His hair looked as though it had been chopped off under a basin. It was jagged and uneven and looked such a mess. Instantly I had a flashback to the convent, to a nun hacking at my lovely long hair with the clippers whilst I cried and pleaded with her to stop. I remembered the cold air on my neck, the feeling of exposure and nakedness.

It had felt like an assault. And now, 17 years later, it had happened to my own child. I could not believe that lightning could strike twice. That fate could be at once so callous and so specific.

Seized with a disproportionate rage, I took his hand and I marched out in the street to find my neighbour.

"Nobody touches my children! Nobody cuts their hair!" I screamed.

The woman and her children cowered in alarm. They were more shocked than scared, I could see that. And I did not blame them for it. I was so angry, I was upsetting myself. But I could not help it. I was back at the convent, defending Freddie, comforting Johnny, standing up for one of my own.

It was an instinct, a basic urge.

"Don't touch a hair on his head ever again!" I yelled.

And then I slammed back into the house and cried tears of shame and regret, knowing that my tantrum had little to do with the neighbour and everything to do with Sister Isobel.

On another occasion, other neighbours complained about Lee playing football on open ground near our houses. They didn't like the noise. They didn't like the nuisance. They didn't like my children, that was what it boiled down to, I was sure of it.

Again, I was zoomed back in time to the convent, and saw a pitiful little girl, stuck inside in the Reccy, wishing she could play outside. I saw a long, bony finger poking in her face telling her to be quiet, telling her not to ask questions, telling her she had no name.

I rapped on the neighbour's door, my temper steaming and my eyes blazing.

"My son is allowed to play out. He is allowed to be happy," I snapped furiously. "Don't ever try to stop him."

Again, I was over-reacting. But I was a wounded lioness, protecting her cub, and there is no stronger sensibility.

When I had first given birth to Shane, I had been overwhelmed by the all-consuming, physical pain and joy that is motherhood. But I had felt also a stab of worry and paranoia.

What if I was to follow in my own mother's footsteps? What if I was to inherit her curse? She had suffered with a mental illness so debilitating that it had prevented her looking after her own children. It had stopped her from being a mother.

I knew, as I cradled my baby boy in my arms, smelled the newness of his scalp, and felt the softness of his skin, that I would not be able to cope if it happened to me. Giving birth had left me vulnerable, as though I had been cracked open, like a nut, and all my deepest emotions were exposed.

I had resolved to be strong. To be focussed and to be fierce. I was present, I was in the moment always. Yet this vigilance, this over-motherliness, was threatening my relationship with my children, just as my mother's illness had with hers.

The trigger in each situation was different. But the casualties each time were the children.

Whilst trying to protect my little ones, I was slowly driving them away. There was tragedy in the irony – and it broke my heart.

It was a constant battle to keep my children physically and emotionally close to me. And during those efforts, though I did not at first see it, my marriage was falling apart. I tried, as I'm sure Bill did, to make things work.

But somehow my words sounded more accusatorial than friendly, and the distance between us just grew. But I felt sure he wouldn't leave me – because that would mean leaving his babies. In his way, he loved them, as I did, in mine.

Besides, they were too beautiful to leave behind, I told myself. There was no way he could do it. I would kiss my three children each morning and marvel that these little cherubs were mine. Ours.

But one evening, in 1976, I was full of a cold and running a temperature. I had already cooked for Bill and the children and was struggling to find the energy to get myself out of the house, to go and check on my dad and the rest of the family.

"Why don't you stay the night there, save you trailing home here in the dark?" Bill suggested. "I can look after the kiddies, just for one night.

"You need a good night's sleep, too. You're exhausted. Stay at your dad's Marie, I promise you I can cope."

I didn't like the thought of being away from my children, but I was touched by Bill's thoughtfulness. So, I thanked him and agreed.

Back at the old family home, I cooked a meal, washed up and did some housework. And with all the activity, I started to feel a bit better.

"You know, I think I'll go back home, after all," I told dad. "I'll miss my babies if I stay here overnight."

Dad walked me home. But as we got to the front door, and he said goodnight, I stopped suddenly in my tracks. I could hear Rod Stewart blasting out from the bedroom. And my hackles rose. I knew something was going on.

Quietly, I crept into the house and up the stairs. I had a bottle of milk in my hand. I pushed open the bedroom door, and there was Bill, in bed with a woman I recognised from the local pub.

It was a sucker punch.

"You bastard!" I screamed, lunging at him and smashing him over the head with the milk bottle.

The woman tried to flee but I grabbed her and dragged her down the stairs by her arm, yelling and spitting insults at her before I shoved her out, into the street.

"And don't ever come back!" I bawled.

I ran back upstairs, to check the children's bedroom, hoping against hope they were all asleep. To my disgust, they were in bed, fully-clothed. The sight of my children in bed in their outdoor clothes upset me more than anything. That was the worst of it.

Bill slunk off to his mother's house so that she could pick the pieces of glass from his scalp. Though he returned home, for a short period, our days as a family were numbered.

It was not long after Lee's fourth birthday, in August 1977, when we separated. Despite everything, I was stunned. I had believed that we could make a go of it, for the sake of our lovely children. But I had been wrong. My main concern, apart from the children, was money. I was not working and I had no way of paying the rent. I was panic-stricken that I would be out on the streets with my brood. I went without food, so that they could eat. I went to bed when they did, to save on lighting and heating. I struggled from day to day.

The children started school, but I refused to send them to the local Catholic primary. I didn't want them anywhere near nuns. I couldn't take the risk of history repeating itself.

I made sure there was a party and a celebration for every birthday, for my siblings, and for their children, too.

When we sang *Happy Birthday* my voice was louder than most, because I had many lost years to make up for.

They were happy times.

But I also had dark days where I felt fragile and weak, and I was shrouded in a fog of depression. And during those times, my children suffered. I found it hard to even make out their faces through the gloom.

I was not the perfect parent I had strived to be. I made mistakes and my bond with my children was certainly frayed and damaged because if it.

I had wanted to package up the past and dump it somewhere far away. But instead, it peered over my shoulder constantly, it festered and oozed like a sore, it threatened to engulf me and drag me under.

I suffered. Worse still, my children suffered. It was a huge regret to me. I wanted to tell my children that I was sorry. I wanted to explain myself. But the words did not come easily to me.

And when Lee's sixth birthday came around, a chill went through me. He was the same age as I had been, when I was sent to the convent. He was just a little boy, a scrap of a kid.

How on earth had my parents been able to send me away? And how had I survived it? I wanted to hug Lee close, to tell him how much I loved him, to make sure he knew he was precious. But I had learned, growing up, that close physical contact was to be feared. And that skewed and neurotic misconception was passed on, right through my relationship with my own children.

I loved them dearly, but I found it hard to show it.

The memories of the convent troubled me more and more at those times. I was fiercely and irrationally possessive.

A couple of times, I was called into school by Lee's teacher. He had been messing around in assembly, apparently being silly while the choir was performing.

The teacher was a nice woman and she was only trying to help.

But seeing her stand over Lee, her finger waggling, her jaw moving up and down, I felt a fury rising within me.

"Don't speak to my son like that!" I yelled. "He's done nothing wrong!"

I couldn't accept that my son could, or should, ever be disciplined. It was not good for them, I knew that. It was my failing, as a mother.

Even in the street, if I saw children being told off, it would upset me. I hated any kind of aggression and yet conversely, I was aware that I could be aggressive myself. Sometimes, in an instant, I was overcome by an extra-ordinary and extreme anger and I did not understand why. I was always wary, too, of anyone in authority: priests, doctors, teachers. And nuns. Nuns above all else.

Chapter Twenty Five

One afternoon in April 1980, we went to visit my sister, Teresa, who lived nearby, as she had just given birth to her first daughter. When we arrived, I spotted an American car outside.

"Ooh, she's got a posh visitor with a fancy car," I said.

It turned out that the owner of the car was a man called Jack Hargreaves. He was a friend of Teresa's and he had a nice camera. He had called in to take a photo of her and her new baby.

"A fancy camera as well!" I smiled.

Jack was a lovely man; kind, gentle and with a slow, genuine smile. He was tall and slim with wavy, shoulder length, blonde hair. He told me he owned a garage, fixing and selling motorbikes.

He was a bright and intelligent man, too.

Before we left, I whispered to Teresa: "Ask Jack if he will take me out for a drink!"

It was only half a joke. I hadn't been for a night out for years, and I felt that I had clicked with Jack. I had a feeling about him.

I was standing on the doorstep, ready to leave, when Teresa asked him, and he exclaimed: "Yes, of course, I'd love to!"

And that was that. We went out that week, and we had the time of our lives. Jack held my hand all night and I felt young and silly again. Little did I know, but we would be holding hands for the next 30 years.

I was falling for him, head over heels. My heart was his, right from that first weekend. All through my teenage years, I had scoffed at my friends' crushes on pop-stars and pin-ups. Now, I had my very own real-life heart throb! I had a lightness in my chest, and a sparkle in my eyes.

Jack seemed almost too good to be true.

But a few months on, I reached crisis point. I received an eviction notice and we were about to be officially homeless. I had no money left.

"What are we going to do?" I fretted.

I was too proud to mention it to Jack. But that weekend, he turned up to see me and told me he was planning to move house himself. He'd been to view a new flat with a balcony.

"That's nice," I replied, hardly able to concentrate on what he was saying.

"Problem is," he said. "I don't want a new house of my own. I want to live here, with you."

I sucked in my breath.

"I'm being evicted," I told him sadly. "I'm behind with the rent. You can't move in here."

Jack didn't say too much. He went home and later that day, I was surprised to see him at the door again.

"Here," he said, putting £500 cash on my dining table. "Go and pay your arrears. Don't argue. It's a gift, not a loan."

My jaw dropped. I almost collapsed in shock. I had never seen that amount of money. I was protesting and thanking him all at once, crying, laughing and whooping.

The rent was paid. Jack moved in. And at last I had the safety and security I had craved all of my life. We were happier than I could have imagined possible.

Jack worked hard at his garage. I got a job at the market. He never raised his voice or his fist to anyone, but he was the bravest and the toughest man I knew.

With a little more money to spare, I was able to buy treats for us all. In the school holidays, we had days out.

"Can we go to Blackpool, mum?" Lee pleaded. "Please."

The idea left me reeling. Blackpool. It only took one word and there I was, a frightened, mixed-up little girl. It was as though I had a Tardis, flipping me in and out of the decades, reliving the grotesque details of my childhood.

"Course we can," I smiled. "We'll get the train."

We ran along the beach and across the piers, we collected pebbles and shells. We had ice-creams and candyfloss.

"I love it here, mum," he laughed, facing into the wind as it blew him backwards across the sand.

I was determined not to let the past in. It had ruined one childhood. It would not ruin my children's. But when I saw the line of seafront guest houses, my eyes misted over. I could see the ghost of myself, standing shy and confused at Elizabeth's door.

"Which one?" she had asked, pointing to her bottles of nail polish. "I'd like your opinion."

It was pitiful but also wonderful, that her kindness had meant so much to me. I wished I could have let her know. I wished so much could have been different. But I counted myself lucky that I was going home to a man who loved me.

I hovered between the past and the present, between the horror and the happiness. And Jack could see it. He knew the same old film was playing in my mind. And he knew he had never seen it.

"Tell me about the convent," he would say to me. "Tell me what happened to you."

But I knew how sensitive he was, and I didn't want to upset him.

"It was dreadful," was all I could manage. "Really dreadful."

A part of me didn't want our relationship sullied and spoiled with the poison from the past. Jack's love was genuine and pure. I didn't want to muddy up the two.

One night, as we lay on the couch together, I said to Jack: "Have you any regrets?"

And he replied: "Only that I didn't meet you sooner."

It was such a lovely thing to say and it took me right back to the playground, to the little boy who had been my light, my hope, through those troubled years.

"There was a boy at school who once told me he would even go to Africa to be with me," I told Jack.

Jack smiled.

"And so would I," he replied. "Always remember that, Marie."

This was the happiness and stability I had waited for all my life. Jack and I were rarely apart. People would tease us for holding hands everywhere we went.

"You're like two love-birds," they smiled.

But it was impossible for me to erase the memories from the convent. They were like a hangover, a dull, throbbing reminder of something rotten. I was reminded of the abuse every morning, when I opened my wardrobe and unhooked my clothes from their coat-hangers.

For many years, I'd been unable even to have coat-hangers in my house. For me, they were weapons. Objects of torture. But then, as my children got a little bigger, they needed hangers for school blazers and shirts. And Jack needed coat-hangers for his suits and smart shirts.

And so, eventually, I choked back my fears and I relented. But I felt like I was inviting the enemy into my home. It helped that, over time, plastic hangers replaced wooden ones. They looked and sounded less malevolent, and gradually my flashbacks eased.

On my ironing days, I would carry a huge pile of coat-hangers downstairs, ready for the freshly pressed clothes. And it was inevitable that once or twice, I dropped the lot, and they fell to the floor with a clatter.

Just the noise of the coat hangers, and the shapes they made as they fell; the sharp angles and the unforgiving edges, was enough to propel me, like a rocket, back to the convent. In an instant, I was a quivering, bewildered, little girl again.

"I'm sorry," I told Jack, covering my face and gulping back my tears.

But though Jack knew nothing of my trauma, he understood me nonetheless and his patience was endless. He would wipe away my tears, take my hand in his and say:

"Remember, I would go to Africa to look for you."

And it was enough to make me gather up the hangers, switch on the iron and carry on. It was enough to make me smile again, if only on the outside.

* * *

It was a long time before I finally plucked up courage to share more with Jack about what I had been through. One night, as we had our tea together, I said:

"The nuns in the convent never used my name, Jack. Not once. They called me Kibby."

Jack's knife and fork dropped onto the table with a clang and he stared at me, pain and shock in his eyes.

"That's the most horrible thing I ever heard," he said.

Chapter Twenty Five

He was so upset, he didn't even finish the stew I'd cooked for him. And I knew I could not tell him anymore. He cared too much, he was too invested in me, to hear the truth.

I'd had one husband who didn't love me enough to listen to my troubles. And another who loved me too much. I was beginning to fear that my secrets from the convent would go to the grave with me, and that I would carry them around for the rest of my life.

Chapter Twenty Six

My siblings grew up, settled down, and had families of their own. Freddie struggled, always, as anyone in his shoes would. He drank too much, to try to blot out the memories of his childhood. Alcohol became a crutch for him. And it also became his downfall.

I was especially close to Teresa and, of course, to lovely Johnny. He was a flamboyant, extravert young man. He wore exotic, outlandish clothes, and would often dress head to toe in white. With his little round glasses, and his off-beat ways, he reminded everyone of John Lennon.

Johnny loved to dance, too. He was always surrounded by gaggles of boys and girls.

"They're your fans," I used to tell him, with a smile. "Just like the Beatles."

For a while, he lived with Jack and I, but then he went off to Birmingham university to study psychology. I was bursting with pride. Of the whole family, he was certainly the most intelligent. I rarely saw him without a book under his arm.

But university didn't suit Johnny and he was soon back home and in a rented flat, just outside Manchester. I noticed that he was going out more and more and I suspected he was partying too much and playing too hard.

One day late in 1982, the police called me and told me they had found Johnny dead, in his living room. It was thought he had over-dosed accidentally on prescription drugs and alcohol.

I was broken-hearted. I had always thought of him, when he was young, as a little like Jesus. I had worried that he was too angelic, too special, for this world. And I had been right.

I brought his body home, into my living room, with an open coffin, so that I could give him one last cuddle. His funeral was packed out. Everyone had loved Johnny.

Afterwards, I missed him terribly. I could recall vividly the scene in the convent. His screams, his chubby hands around my neck, his big eyes filled with tears.

It had torn me apart to let him go once. And now, I had to do it again.

The sadness was debilitating, but Jack was wonderful. On darker days, he would remind me:

"I'm here for you, Marie. And I'll go to Africa for you, if needs be."

* * *

Ten years after Johnny's death, tragedy struck once more.

Dad had been unwell for a while, unsteady on his feet, pale-faced and weak. He was 79 years old and he had never seen a doctor in all the years I could remember. But one morning, in the spring of 1992, I called to see him and I felt worried. He was clammy and a little short of breath, and he had no energy at all. By now, he was living alone in a flat, a short walk away from me.

I rang his GP and the receptionist told me, very curtly, that they were too busy to see him.

"But I think he's really ill," I told her. "He's never seen a doctor before but now he needs one."

"If he's so ill, you should call an ambulance," she replied.

Dad wouldn't hear of me calling an ambulance. He didn't like a fuss. So I made him a brew and some toast, which he hardly touched, and I promised to call him later that day.

That same afternoon, I was due at my word processing class. I was doing a course to help me at work, and I was enjoying it. But, as I got to the top of my street, I suddenly had an instinct. Without really thinking about it, I changed direction and went to knock on dad's door. When he didn't reply, I started to fret.

A neighbour came out, a lovely man who lived in the flat above, and he offered to climb in through dad's open bathroom window. A few moments later, through the window, his voice came, urgent and panicky. They were the words I had been dreading.

"I'm sorry Marie, your dad's on the floor, it doesn't look good."

He let me into the flat and I rushed over to check on dad. But it was too late. He was gone, after a massive heart attack. Again, I organised the funeral, with an open coffin at my house, so that we could all say goodbye. Now, at 38 years old, just as when I was six, I was the one taking responsibility, making sure everyone else was all right.

"I'm here, dad," I said softly, as I gave him one last kiss goodbye. "Your right hand man. I'm holding the fort."

It hit me too, that now – at long last – I was indeed an orphan. Wicked old Sister Isobel had got her way in the end.

I missed my parents, and Johnny, so much. But Jack was with me, through every stage of my grief, and carrying the burden together made it so much easier.

Chapter Twenty Seven

With my three children growing up and settling down with their own families, Jack and I had more time to spend together. And one evening, after work, Jack came into the living room and put an envelope on the table.

"Tickets," he announced, with a twinkle in his eye. "We're off to Portugal on holiday!"

My eyes widened with a mixture of excitement and alarm. Holidays would always have a sinister connotation for me. Holiday was synonymous with horror in my mind. I couldn't help thinking back to the day I'd left for the convent.

When my dad had said: "You're going on a holiday." I saw my six-year-old self, jumping into the back of the social workers' car, and my heart bled. But I knew that this time, for certain, it was different. I could trust Jack like I trusted nobody else in the world. I forced my grimace into a smile and flung my arms around him.

"Thank you," I smiled.

It was my first trip abroad, save the ferry to Ireland, all those years previously. And this holiday, unlike the first, lived up to and surpassed all expectations.

As Jack and I lay on the beach, sipping our ice-cold cocktails and soaking up the sun, I felt close to paradise.

"It was a lovely thought, bringing me away on holiday," I told him. "Thank you."

Jack turned to me and winked.

"That's nothing," he replied. "I'd go to Portugal for you – I'd even go to Africa. You should know that by now!"

* * *

Dad had been dead six years when, one morning in 1998, I opened the door to find two police officers standing there.

"We're here as part of Operation Cleopatra," they told me.

I looked blankly at them. It meant nothing to me.

"We're investigating historical child abuse," they explained. "We think we might be able to help you."

I felt my stomach drop right down into my slippers. Gripping the doorframe, I shivered as flashes from the past, one after another, zoomed past my eyeline, like a film on fast forward. The Reccy. The washrooms. The tiny cell-like rooms. The bigger girls. The littler girls. And the nuns.

"Can we come in?" asked one of the officers.

I nodded weakly, taking measured breaths, trying to slow my heart down. Jack was in the living room and as he saw my face blanche, he looked up in alarm.

"What's going on?" he asked.

The officers explained they wanted to ask me about one nun in particular. Sister Isobel O'Brien. It was the first time I had ever heard her full name.

"O'Brien?" I repeated faintly. "Yes, I'm pretty sure I know who you mean."

She was, they explained, the nun in charge of the girls at Greenfield House, our Lady's Convent, in Billinge, Lancashire.

"The convent was run by nuns from the Sisters Of Charity of St Paul the Apostle," added one of the officers.

I almost spat my coffee out. It would have been funny had it not been so cruel.

"There was not much charity there," I muttered darkly. "Not much at all."

St Paul was best known to me for his letters in the New Testament about love, patience and hope. The irony was horrific.

But I was curious to know how the police had found me – and how they knew about the abuse.

"There have been other complaints against Sister O'Brien," said one of the officers. "Other children suffered. We had a look at the records from the convent. And that is what brought us to you."

My blood ran cold. All these years, I had thought I was the only one. In some ways, it was a relief to know that I had not been singled out. That I was not in some way a bad or an unlovable child, as I had sometimes feared. It was a comfort, too, to know that there were people on my side, people who understood.

But it was, more than anything, a devastating blow to learn that other children had suffered as I had. I would not have wished that lonely torment on any other child. The thought of another little Marie, sobbing and smarting as I had, was heart-breaking.

I held my head in my hands and cried.

"Don't upset yourself, love," Jack said gently. "Please."

The officers wanted me to tell them about the convent. And I wanted so much to help. But in front of Jack, it was impossible. I knew he felt my pain almost as much as I did, and I could not bear to tell them everything. I worried it might ruin him.

It had been so long, too. I had never in my life confided in anyone about the level of physical and sexual violence I had endured. The words got stuck, like a peach stone, lodged in my throat, blocking the way. I couldn't get them out – but I couldn't push them back in either.

"I'm sorry," I told the officers. "I've done my best."

They gave me information too. Snippets from other statements.

"Some children were made to lie in bed with their arms crossed over the sheets," they said. "Was it like that for you, too?"

I shook my head. But they had struck a nerve.

"Not quite," I replied. "But I had to join my hands and keep the sheets straight. Sister Isobel didn't like to have the sheets creased."

The officers promised to come back to me, with more information, in the future.

After the police had gone, Jack was unusually quiet and thoughtful.

"I know you have more to tell," he told me, softly. "I want to help you. Remember – I'm on your side. I will go to Africa for you. I will go to the ends of the earth."

I nodded and smiled. But this time, Jack's love and support alone was not enough. The bogeyman was out of the box. And I knew it would be impossible now to squash him back inside.

Each night, I had horrible dreams of coat hangers, of slithering, scaly, tongues, of children trapped in window-less rooms. But now, it wasn't just me. There were dozens of us, lined up, naked, waiting helplessly to be picked off and gobbled up, one by one, by a large black bird.

I got up each day, clouded by my nightmares. Each day, I was on tenterhooks. I expected another visit from the police, which I looked forward to and dreaded, in equal measure. I wanted this secret out. But I also wanted it buried.

* * *

One evening, in August 2010, Jack and I were watching TV, holding hands and chatting comfortably. Jack usually had a bath every night at around 9pm and I reminded him that time was getting on.

"I'll go up when this programme finishes," he told me.

Upstairs, I heard him bustling around, and then splashing as he got into the bath.

"Alright love?" I called.

"Aches and pains and old bones," he joked in reply. "But yes, I'm all right."

I watched TV for a while but there was no sign of Jack. He would always, always, come downstairs to kiss me goodnight before going to bed.

At the foot of the stairs, I shouted: "Haven't you been a long time in that bath?"

Silence.

Suddenly, my heart began to beat a bit faster. Why wasn't he answering? I went up one step. And then I stopped. One side of my brain told me that I was about to find my husband dead in the bath. Another side told me not to be so silly.

I forced myself to walk up the rest of the staircase, but it felt like such a long way. My legs were heavy and my hands trembled on the bannister rail.

"Please," I whispered. "No."

Turning the corner, into the bathroom, I hardly dared look. But there he was. My precious Jack. My life-saver, my soul-mate and my redemption. My best friend in the world.

He'd had a heart attack in the bath, aged 70.

As with the deaths in the rest of my family, I insisted on bringing Jack home, with an open coffin. I treasured those last few days, just me and him, in the tranquillity and the security of our own home. I sat for hours next to the coffin, holding his hand, and it was just like the old days. We'd had so much happiness, so much love. And I knew, for that, I had to be grateful.

Before his coffin was closed, I leaned in to give him one last kiss.

"See you in Africa, Jack," I whispered.

After the funeral, I kept his ashes at home, in the same house we had lived in for the whole of our relationship. I felt close to him there.

But losing him was very hard. My grief was raw. Some days I could not face even leaving the house.

And oddly, or perhaps not so, I found solace in the church. Even when Jack was alive, I had sometimes attended Mass, though I could not really explain why. He was not a religious man, but he was happy to come along with me, just for company.

Now, with him gone, I reached out to the church for help. It was a decision which I knew people might struggle to understand. But as time passed, the church became another family for me, a community.

As well as attending mass, I helped out at church, reading the lessons and organising social events. All my life,

I had strived for acceptance and belonging. The church had taken that away from me when I was small. And now, it was handing it all back.

* * *

The year after Jack died, I was watching the evening news, in my armchair, almost dozing off. But the next item had me sitting bolt upright, with my pulse racing.

Being interviewed was a man who had been the victim of abuse in the Catholic care home system. And with him, was his solicitor who was bringing a civil case for victims of abuse.

Scrambling to my feet, I scribbled down the name of the solicitor and I looked him up the next morning. I had heard nothing from the police for years and I wondered if this might be a way forward.

The next day, I called the solicitor and asked for an appointment. To my amazement, he knew all about Sister Isobel O'Brien, just as the police did.

All these years I had imagined she was a secret. My secret. But other people had suffered as I had.

Meeting with my solicitor, reliving the sounds and the smells of Our Lady's Convent, was upsetting, but it was also hugely cathartic.

For the first time, I said it out loud. Sitting in my own living room, with Jack's ashes at my side for moral support,

I spoke about the sexual abuse, about the beatings, about the relentless physical, sexual and mental cruelty which plagued my every moment – waking and sleeping.

I realised, too, as the tears streamed down my cheeks, that the big girls were not responsible for my abuse. Dil certainly was not. Like me, they were children, frightened, vulnerable, lonely and manipulated. They were victims, just as I was.

The real aggressor, the predator in chief, was Sister Isobel herself.

The solicitor explained that my case would be launched against The Trustees of Sisters of Charity of St Paul the Apostle. Sister Isobel was a member of the order. The Archdiocese of Birmingham was handling all safeguarding claims.

But it would be a lengthy process, and more victims, more testimonies, were needed.

"This will take years and years before we reach a resolution," he warned me.

It was frustrating. But all I could do was wait. Again, I tried to push the convent to the back of my mind. But it was like picking a scab; once I had started, I could not stop.

My children could see I wasn't myself.

"What's up, mum?" Lee asked.

I shrugged and managed a smile.

"Ghosts from the past," I told him. "That's all, love."

When the phone call from the police eventually came, in December 2015, it was heart-wrenchingly disappointing.

"Our inquiries show that Sister Isobel has died," said the officer. "We want you to know that, if she had been alive, she would most certainly have faced criminal charges."

It was some small comfort. But, as I replaced the receiver, I couldn't help feeling that she had got away with it. She had ruined so many – how many? – young lives.

My solicitor was in touch soon after, and explained that Sister Isobel's abuse would be classified by the police as a 'detected crime' because she would have been charged with the offences, if she hadn't died.

"The case will still continue against the order of nuns," he told me. "But it will be difficult."

She'd had the last, hollow laugh. And it rang in my ears for months afterwards.

* * *

Over the summer of 2019, I made the decision to face my fears head on. For over 50 years, I had been on the run – from the convent, from my nightmares, from those long, grasping tentacles under my bedsheets.

Enough was enough.

I spoke to the local newspaper and they ran a story, appealing for victims to come forward. To my amazement, two women got in contact that same week.

"We were abused by Sister Isobel O'Brien, at the convent in Liverpool," they said. "She beat us with belts and punched us on the head or in the back with her knuckles.

"She called us names, belittled and humiliated us. She told us nobody wanted us and nobody loved us. We just want you to know that you are not on your own."

More people got in touch. Their stories were harrowing, but they gave me strength, too. I felt as though, together, we could expose the horror. And we could stop it happening again.

And so, in October 2019, I decided to go back there. It was the first time I had even travelled that same route since I was a little girl. But as I stared out of the car windows, the surrounding scenery was unrecognisable to me.

There were new roads, housing estates, petrol stations and factories.

I thought back to the little girl, her face pressed at the window, over-awed by the sight of a sheep. Thrilled at the idea of a holiday.

It was only when we turned into the lane that something caught in my chest.

"Here it is," I whispered.

And then, there it was, glaring down at us. The convent. Much changed and renovated. But unmistakeably and fiercely hostile.

How could I ever have thought this was a holiday camp? I laughed a little at my own naivety. But my only mistake, really, was to believe what I had been told by my father.

And of course, I had wanted desperately to believe it. I had wanted so much to be posh. To be 'someone'. Sad then, that I was taken to a place where I was 'no-one'. Without a name.

The convent was now a school for children with specialist needs, some were day pupils and some residential, and it was a busy hub of noise and activity. But it felt like a happy place, too. The atmosphere had changed. Maybe the convent had been desperate to get rid of Sister Isobel too, just as the children were. Maybe the old bricks had breathed a long sigh of relief when her order finally packed their righteous bags and left.

The receptionist, when I explained who I was, was kind enough to let me walk through the entrance hallway.

The first thing I heard was the sound of a teacher's heels, clackety clack, on the wooden parquet floor. My mouth ran dry and the colour must have drained from my face.

"Are you alright?" asked the receptionist.

I nodded, pushing away the visions that were swirling around my head: the ominous sound of Sister Isobel's shoes, the grotesque cruelty, the intolerable feelings of abandonment, of hopelessness and despair.

"I'm alright," I said confidently. "Or at least, I'm alright now."

I retraced my old steps, running along behind Sister Isobel, and into the Mother Superior's office. The whole place seemed so much smaller, so much less imposing than

I had remembered. Back then, the very walls seemed to ooze evil. Every window pane had a sinister shine. Now, it was a rather friendly place. There were no dark corners, no dirty little secrets.

The corridors were shorter and lighter. The statues had gone into hiding, hanging their heads in shame, no doubt, at the horrors they had witnessed under Sister Isobel's reign.

I had expected to be frightened and alarmed. Or bitter and angry. At the very least, I had imagined I might cry. But in the end, the visit left me only with a sense of enduring sadness. Sadness for a lost child and for a lost childhood.

The school, just down the road, had been knocked down and in its place was a housing estate. But in the local shop I found a woman a little older than me, who remembered the convent well.

"I was in a choir and we used to go in there and sing for the orphans," she told me. "Poor things. They had a real time of it, so I hear. They didn't half suffer, some of those kids.

"But we had no idea back then. And of course, nobody thought to question those nuns. Nobody would have dared."

It all came back to questions. I'd spent half my life asking too many questions and paying the price. And the other half, when it really mattered, I hadn't asked any at all.

That night, in bed, I didn't sleep. The visit to the convent had turned me upside down – once again. But I knew, also, it had been therapeutic. It was about facing the demons of my past and embracing the promise of my future.

With the old wounds disturbed and smarting once again, I made an appointment with a counsellor. My attitudes were changing, very slowly at first, but faster now, away from hiding what had happened. Now, I wanted the world to know.

My counsellor was surprised that I had no anger towards Sister Isobel. None at all.

"Why is that, Marie?" he asked me. "Where does all the blame go?"

It was not easy to explain. But the way I saw it, I had to forgive her for my sake – not hers. What she did to me had eaten away at me for most of my life.

All through my childhood, I had dreaded being abandoned. Even as an adult, I was terrified that I was not wanted or loved. I had lived in fear and in despair and the spectre of Sister Isobel had stalked me like a great, black, malevolent crow. There were times when I felt it might swallow me whole.

The bitterness I felt, after leaving the convent, was corrosive and destructive. And it was pointless, too. I had felt like I was being held captive, as though a part of me, my six-year-old self, was still imprisoned in the convent, and always would be. It would have smothered me to death eventually, if I hadn't burst through and broken free.

Now, this was no longer my burden or my millstone. The shame and the disgust and the guilt all belonged to Sister Isobel. She was welcome to it all.

Over the past 50 years, I had moved on, albeit subconsciously. I was breathing clean air now. I had forgiven her.

Chapter Twenty Eight

At the end of 2019, I made another decision which both divided and shocked my family and friends. I had seen a job advert, in a church magazine, for a priest's housekeeper.

The job was in County Mayo, on the West Coast of Ireland. One weekend I flew to meet the priest, Father Sean, and we got on like a house on fire.

"Will you take the job, Marie?" he asked me.

My three children are grown with families of their own. I have grandchildren and great-grandchildren and they will always mean the world to me.

But I feel now it's time to leave Oldham and to find my peace elsewhere. Jack's ashes, and his love, will travel with me wherever I go. And I will carry baby Shane, and my brother Johnny, in my heart always.

My legal action against the church is moving – very slowly – and I don't want to hook my whole life around it. I don't want to hate anyone, any more. But I do hope that my case might be a positive platform for other victims. I'd like more to come forward as a result of my story.

Strange, I know, that I have launched a legal action against a section of the Catholic Church and yet I'm soon to be working for them, too.

But on the cross, Jesus himself called out: "Father, forgive them, for they do not know what they are doing."

If he could find it in his heart to forgive those who had crucified him, surely I could find it in mine to absolve those who had ruined me.

And so, when Father Sean called me in November 2019, my mind was made up.

"I'll do it," I agreed. "I'll take the job."

My plans are in the early stages, but I'm hoping to move out there in 2020. My kids, my friends, my siblings are totally baffled. But in my mind, it all makes perfect sense.

For me, Sister Isobel has no connection with my faith. True, the Catholic church has threatened to drag me under at times. But it has also kept me afloat. Sister Isobel could never be a part of that.

I ought to be angry with her, perhaps. Instead, I pity her. I feel sorry that her whole life was consumed with the abuse and the torture of little children. If I knew where she was buried, I would like to lay flowers on her grave.

I'd like her to know that I have a home. I have a family. And despite her best efforts, I have found happiness and peace.

She did not destroy me. My name is not Kibby.

Also by Mirror Books

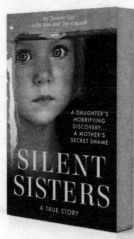

Silent Sisters
Joanne Lee
With Ann and Joe Cusack

A DEADLY SECRET. A HORRIFYING DISCOVERY.

For over 20 years, Joanne Lee's mother kept the remains of her newborn babies hidden in her wardrobe.

Growing up in a chaotic Merseyside household, Joanne suffered neglect and abusive control while her mother lapsed into a downward spiral. But the consequences of her mother's messy lifestyle turned out to be far worse than Joanne could ever have imagined – the family home held a sinister secret.

In Silent Sisters, Joanne, who was falsely accused of murdering her own baby sister, tells her story for the first time – her struggle to piece together the truth and to give four babies the proper burial they deserve.

MIRROR BOOKS

Also by Mirror Books

Wicked Girl

Jeanie Doyle

Jeanie Doyle cares for young and dysfunctional mums, showing them how to care for their newborn babies.

The first in a brand-new series of books by the "foster super-gran", *Wicked Girl* is the shocking true story of a baby girl who was found abandoned on the steps of a church just before Christmas. While the 14-year-old mother was tracked down, Jeanie took her little daughter into her own care. But while she tried to help the two of them heal and bond, the terrible truth about the baby's father was revealed…

Will mother and daughter be reunited, or will the vulnerable young mum make the heartbreaking decision that they are both better off apart?

MIRROR BOOKS